ALSO BY DEREK WALCOTT

POEMS
Selected Poems
The Gulf
Another Life
Sea Grapes
The Star-Apple Kingdom
The Fortunate Traveller
Midsummer
Collected Poems: 1948–1984
The Arkansas Testament
Omeros

PLAYS
Dream on Monkey Mountain and Other Plays
The Joker of Seville and O Babylon!
Remembrance and Pantomime
Three Plays: The Last Carnival;
Beef, No Chicken; A Branch of the Blue Nile

The Odyssey

THE

ODYSSEY

A Stage Version

DEREK

WALCOTT

The Noonday Press

Farrar Straus Giroux

New York

FOR GREG DORAN AND TONY HILL

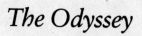

The Odyssey

CHARACTERS

'BLIND' BILLY BLUE, a singer
ODYSSEUS, the Greek general, King of Ithaca
ATHENA, a goddess, also disguised as CAPTAIN MENTES,
    A SHEPHERD, etc.

Ithaca
PENELOPE, wife of Odysseus
TELEMACHUS, son of Odysseus
EURYCLEIA, his old nurse
ANTINOUS, a suitor to Penelope
EURYMACHUS, AMPHINOMUS, CTESIPPUS, LEODES and
    POLYBUS, suitors
MELANTHO, a maid
EUMAEUS, an old swineherd
ARNAEUS, a lout

Pylos
NESTOR, King of Pylos

Sparta
MENELAUS, King of Sparta
HELEN, his wife

PROTEUS, the Old Man of the Sea

The Ship
EURYLOCHUS, Odysseus' lieutenant
ELPENOR, the helmsman
STRATIS, COSTA, STAVROS and TASSO, Odysseus' crew

Scheria
NAUSICAA, a princess
ALCINOUS, her father, King of the Phaeacians
ANEMONE and CHLOE, Phaeacian girls

The Island of the Cyclops
CYCLOPS
A PHILOSOPHER
TWO PATROLMEN
RAM, a manservant

The Island of Calypso
CIRCE, a witch
REVELLERS and CELEBRANTS

The Underworld
ANTICLEA, Odysseus' mother
TIRESIAS
AGAMEMNON, ACHILLES, THERSITES and AJAX,
    the ghosts of Troy

Suitors, Attendants, Maids, Sailors, Mermaids,
    Courtiers, Athletes, etc.

The play was produced by the Royal Shakespeare Company, Stratford-upon-Avon, at The Other Place, 2 July 1992, with the following cast:

ODYSSEUS	Ron Cook
PENELOPE	Amanda Harris
TELEMACHUS	Stephen Casey
EURYCLEIA	Claire Benedict
EUMAEUS	Trevor Martin
ATHENA	Susan-Jane Tanner
BILLY BLUE	Rudolph Walker
ANTINOUS	Jonathan Cake
NESTOR	David Westhead
THERSITES	Gordon Case
PROTEUS	Antony Bunsee
NAUSICAA	Sophie Okonedo
CYCLOPS	Geoffrey Freshwater
CIRCE	Bella Enahoro
ANTICLEA	Darlene Johnson
ACHILLES	Peter de Jersey

Other parts played by members of the cast.

Director	Gregory Doran
Designer	Michael Pavelka

ACT ONE

PROLOGUE

Sound of surf.

BILLY BLUE (*Sings*)
　Gone sing 'bout that man because his stories please us,
　Who saw trials and tempests for ten years after Troy.

　I'm Blind Billy Blue, my main man's sea-smart Odysseus,
　Who the God of the Sea drove crazy and tried to destroy.

　Andra moi ennepe mousa polutropon hos mala polla . . .
　The shuttle of the sea moves back and forth on this line,

　All night, like the surf, she shuttles and doesn't fall
　Asleep, then her rosy fingers at dawn unstitch the design.

　When you hear this chord
　(*Chord*)
　　　　　　　　　　　Look for a swallow's wings,
　A swallow arrowing seaward like a messenger

　Passing smoke-blue islands, happy that the kings
　Of Troy are going home and its ten years' siege is over.

　So my blues drifts like smoke from the fire of that war,
　Cause once Achilles was ashes, things sure fell apart.

　Slow-striding Achilles, who put the hex on Hector
　A swallow twitters in Troy. That's where we start.
　(*Exit.*)

Troy. Dusk. Heavy smoke. The kings, AGAMEMNON,
MENELAUS *and* NESTOR, *with* AJAX *and* THERSITES, *the*
mercenary, pile weapons on a pyre. Drums.

AGAMEMNON
Pile our worn weapons on this remembering cairn.

NESTOR
Till salt air rusts them, till they're wrapped in veils of sand.

MENELAUS
Turn the gaping beaks of our fleet homeward again.

AJAX
Since Troy is a plain of ashes where kites ascend.

THERSITES
Till men ask 'Was it here?' of the gliding frigate.

AGAMEMNON
'Was it here that their lances pinned Achilles' pyre?'

NESTOR
Who rattles his angry lance along heaven's gate.

AGAMEMNON
Through the length of war, home was our long desire.

MENELAUS
It was mine, Menelaus, whose wife was its cause.

AJAX
And mine, Ajax, the heir of Achilles' armour.
(ODYSSEUS *enters at a distance.*)

ODYSSEUS
What?

THERSITES
       Not mine, Thersites. No wife, no son, no house.

AGAMEMNON
And ingenious Odysseus.

NESTOR
             And mine, Nestor.
(*Pause. A swallow twitters overhead. They look up.*)

MENELAUS
That swallow's eager to leave. Where's Odysseus?
THERSITES
In his tent, checking his tribute.
AJAX
                                    Once more, we wait.
(ODYSSEUS *steps forward, eating.*)
AGAMEMNON
We're piling gifts on Achilles' mound. Any size.
(ODYSSEUS *pays his small tribute.*)
ODYSSEUS
There. I couldn't choose what to give. Sorry I'm late.
(*Silence.*)
O lucky dead, who can't tell friends from enemies!
(*Silence.*)
Agamemnon denied you flame-haired Briseis.
(*Silence.*)
Menelaus mocked you: 'Deliverer from Mice'.
(*Silence.*)
Now all your glories are reflected in their eyes.
NESTOR
This scrolled shield Hephaestus hammered, who is its heir?
(*He holds up a shield.*)
THERSITES
He willed it to Odysseus on the battlefield.
AJAX
Achilles was fitful. He promised me first.
ODYSSEUS
                                    Where?
AJAX
Look, two claims injure his spirit! You take the shield.
ODYSSEUS
No, no, you take it, Ajax, you fought the hardest.
AJAX
You heard me say that? Did I ever make that boast?

MENELAUS

For God's sake, it's his burial mound. Let him rest.
(*He gives* ODYSSEUS *the shield.*)

AJAX

Bear it, you turtle! Take ten years to reach your coast.

AGAMEMNON

Now let the coiled rams' horns moan with our departure.

MENELAUS

Let the eagle's pennon steer us through the cloud's foam.
(*Horns and drums.*)

AGAMEMNON

Let these pennons tatter after ten years of war.

NESTOR

Let wet-heeled Athena race our lunging ships home.
(*Exit except* THERSITES *and* ODYSSEUS, *who retrieves
more souvenirs from the mound.*)

THERSITES

So. We're naked men again. Our armour is shelled.

ODYSSEUS

Yes. Home to the fig tree's shade, the wine press, the farm.

THERSITES

Hang it on a hook, but cries will ring from that shield.

ODYSSEUS

How'll you live?

THERSITES

                This old war-dog? Off scraps of fame.

ODYSSEUS

You regret victory, Thersites. I know why.

THERSITES

Yeah? Then you make my dissatisfaction exact.

ODYSSEUS

After victory what?

THERSITES

                Peace. Screw peace. No money.

ODYSSEUS

Peace ruins mercenaries.

THERSITES
                    No? I'll note the fact.
ODYSSEUS
It loosens the bonds of war. That's what you're feeling.
THERSITES
And of course you think you know what my unrest is.
ODYSSEUS
A warm white back curled against you. Your own ceiling.
THERSITES
The sky is my roof. This sword sleeps with Thersites.
ODYSSEUS
Get a son.
THERSITES
                    And a dog. And a blooming garden.
ODYSSEUS
Come to Ithaca.
THERSITES
                    Can you promise me a war?
ODYSSEUS
No. Hang your sword on a hook.
THERSITES
                              What? Hang my own wife?
ODYSSEUS
Our ribbed bodies long for their original shore.
THERSITES
Except this body. That's found no shore to believe.
ODYSSEUS
Lend me your wife, your sword. Here's my will, Thersites.
(THERSITES *gives his sword to* ODYSSEUS, *who draws on
the sand.*)
THERSITES
My white ribs, a harp that the sea-crab's fingers pluck.
ODYSSEUS
My shoal-pebbled island, too stony for horses.
THERSITES
Except Thersites loves horses. His usual luck.

ODYSSEUS

I bequeath him Mount Neriton's marching poplars.

THERSITES

I'd tell them to halt, man. Trees spread peace. I decline.

ODYSSEUS

You'd rule next to me.

THERSITES

                        I'd piss on the populace.

(ODYSSEUS *draws on the sand.*)

ODYSSEUS

Take my hunting dog, Argus.

THERSITES

                           That's it! I resign.

ODYSSEUS

Why?

THERSITES

             Hate dogs. Slobberers. Dumb pain, dumb affection.

ODYSSEUS

Open the gates of those locked teeth. Admit love, friend.

THERSITES

I'll say it with grinding jaw. I loved you. Go on.
(*They embrace, then exit in opposite directions.*
A distant roar, growing. Banners, masts.
BILLY BLUE *enters.*)

BILLY BLUE

Then, as the slow forest of Greek masts began sailing,
(*A long cry of a bird or woman.*)
They heard the wide cry of a woman or frigate bird . . .

And that cry lanced their hearts for all that it augured:
Over the stones of her children, Hecuba wailing.

A funeral cry like a torn cloth, then a huge hum,
The wings of flapping standards unfurling like cranes.

CHORUS OF ARMIES (*Off*)

Ranks and divisions, hoist our banners for home!

BILLY BLUE
Like cranes that darken the sky before winter rains
CHORUS OF ARMIES
The bones of our comrades rattle like dice on this shore.
Ranks from Pylos, divisions from Ida, shapely men.
BILLY BLUE
Their white ribs hoisting the black sail of the vulture.
CHORUS OF ARMIES
Divisions from Aspledon, ranks of poplars fallen.
BILLY BLUE
Then, a sail, for ten years crawling on the sea's line.
(*Exits.*)

SCENE II

Ithaca, ten years later. TELEMACHUS, *seated, is staring at
another chair.* EURYCLEIA *enters with wine, waits.*

TELEMACHUS
A swallow spoke to me from the wrist of that chair.
EURYCLEIA
You send for wine? What happen to your sea captain?
TELEMACHUS
The elect can take natural shapes, Eurycleia.
EURYCLEIA
Lord, bird t'ief this boy's wits.
TELEMACHUS
                                  It twittered, 'He'll return.'
EURYCLEIA
These thoughts is like straw, whirling around your father.
TELEMACHUS
The whirr of one swallow starts destruction's engine.
EURYCLEIA
An' this nest empty. This house that he should be in.

TELEMACHUS
You said Athena, the sea-eyed, is Egyptian.
EURYCLEIA
But never in life me call any bird captain.
TELEMACHUS
She said she'd argued with God to save my father.
EURYCLEIA
Nancy stories me tell you and Hodysseus.
TELEMACHUS
I believe them now. My faith has caught a fever.
EURYCLEIA
Launching your lickle cradles into dreaming seas.
TELEMACHUS
What were those stories? An old slave's superstition?
EURYCLEIA
People don't credit them now. Them too civilize.
TELEMACHUS
It had a girl's voice.
EURYCLEIA (*Laughing*)
A girl? So that's your distraction!
TELEMACHUS
Why?
EURYCLEIA
A girl make sense. But when bird mater'alize . . .
TELEMACHUS
He was trim and bearded and far too young for Troy.
EURYCLEIA
Troy old as you, Telemachus. Twenty years' pain!
TELEMACHUS
She's here, Eurycleia!
EURYCLEIA
I old. Don't mock me, boy!
TELEMACHUS
Believe me!
EURYCLEIA
My faith gone. It can't come back again.

8

TELEMACHUS

To me and my father you have been slave and nurse.

EURYCLEIA

Yes. Is Egypt who cradle Greece till Greece mature.

TELEMACHUS

Then why doubt the goddess now in a swallow's noise?

EURYCLEIA

Well, if that bird was your captain, make him stand there.

(*A sea captain,* CAPTAIN MENTES, *appears.*)

TELEMACHUS

Your faith has returned.

(EURYCLEIA *turns.*)

EURYCLEIA

Forgive my sins, sir. You is?

CAPTAIN MENTES

Your sins are so far back God has forgotten them.

EURYCLEIA

Eurycleia. Me raise both boys.

TELEMACHUS

This is Captain Mentes.

CAPTAIN MENTES

I swam Troy's smoke with his father, that clouded time.

EURYCLEIA

Why you come only now?

CAPTAIN MENTES

Because he's in danger.

EURYCLEIA

This boy come of age. Them suitors don't want no heir.

CAPTAIN MENTES

Strange things may happen here, but there will be stranger.

TELEMACHUS

A swallow has lanced us with light, Eurycleia.

EURYCLEIA

I looking at God and can't remember my sins.

TELEMACHUS

I turned my back. We were talking. Then you weren't there.

9

CAPTAIN MENTES
    I went to the window. My ship is loading bronze.
    (*A roar from the* SUITORS.)
TELEMACHUS
    You can hear for yourself.
CAPTAIN MENTES
                            What's all the feasting for?
TELEMACHUS
    What else? My mother's marriage and my father's wake.
EURYCLEIA
    They go spew like vomit through the gorge of that door.
CAPTAIN MENTES
    You've come of age. You know what you must undertake.
EURYCLEIA
    A hundred boars jostling to nose his mother's trough.
TELEMACHUS
    Grunting and shoving till she finishes her shroud.
EURYCLEIA
    Is a hundred in there, Captain. Plenty enough.
TELEMACHUS
    My father is lost. My faith has entered a cloud.
CAPTAIN MENTES
    He'll fix them. His bow-string humming like a swallow.
TELEMACHUS
    I can't leave my mother with them. It isn't right.
CAPTAIN MENTES
    Look, the day she chooses, you die. You must leave now.
EURYCLEIA
    She will choose one.
CAPTAIN MENTES
                        Then he'll murder you one night.
    (*Enter drunken* SUITORS – ANTINOUS, EURYMACHUS,
    AMPHINOMUS, CTESIPPUS *and* LEODES – *dragging* BILLY
    BLUE *and* MAIDS *with them.*)
AMPHINOMUS
    What's the boy doing here? This stuff's not for you, lad!

(*A food fight, they pelt* TELEMACHUS.)

EURYMACHUS
We'll keep doing this till we hear from your mother.

CTESIPPUS
Who's your friend?
(*They crowd* TELEMACHUS *and* MENTES.)

AMPHINOMUS
      Can't you see the kid's missing his dad?

EURYMACHUS
Your dad's dead. You'll choose one of us for another.
(*Silence.*)

CAPTAIN MENTES
Why are they suddenly quiet?

TELEMACHUS
      For my mother.
(*The* SUITORS *draw back, stumbling. Light from an open door.* PENELOPE, *veiled, crosses.*)

CAPTAIN MENTES
They part like hills for a sail entering harbour.

TELEMACHUS
They are stunned by her passage each time she appears.

EURYCLEIA
She begging the poet to stop praising the war.
(*The* SUITORS *jostle, crowding* PENELOPE.)

AMPHINOMUS
Aim for my heart! Arch that white arm!

EURYMACHUS
      It's been three years.

CTESIPPUS
Not Leodes. His sex is soft wax. It'd dissolve!

LEODES
Not vain Ctesippus, plucking his brows in mirrors!

CTESIPPUS
Little shrimp prick!

LEODES
    His own face is all he can love.

EURYMACHUS
Unveil the shrine of that brow to its worshippers!

CTESIPPUS
Those eyes, black olives, that forehead whose marble stuns!
(PENELOPE *unveils her face.*)

AMPHINOMUS
Her smile is like the sunlight edging a window.

CTESIPPUS
Till it brightens Antinous, her favoured prince.
(PENELOPE, BILLY BLUE *and* MAIDS, *except* MELANTHO,
exit. TELEMACHUS *crosses to the* SUITORS.)

TELEMACHUS
I mourned my father's absence. Soon I'll avenge it!

CTESIPPUS
Such sweet impetuosity, Telemachus!

EURYMACHUS
There's a hundred of us, boy. How will you manage it?

TELEMACHUS
Pigs! From today you will stop uprooting my house!
(*The* SUITORS *exit.*)

CAPTAIN MENTES
Steer for the wide sands of Pylos. Look for Nestor.

TELEMACHUS
Right now?

CAPTAIN MENTES
Next, Sparta. Find red-haired Menelaus.

TELEMACHUS
Those are two long journeys, Captain. What's the quest
for?

CAPTAIN MENTES
Do you want your father's shadow to cross this house?

TELEMACHUS
God!

CAPTAIN MENTES
I've twenty oarsmen waiting, hunched on their oars.

TELEMACHUS
One for each year I've missed him. Manning whose vessel?
CAPTAIN MENTES
A beaked yellow ship, like a hawk? Antinous'.
TELEMACHUS
You seized it?
CAPTAIN MENTES
Borrowed it. Well, it was there to seize.
TELEMACHUS
And it's fitted?
CAPTAIN MENTES
With amphora of ground barley.
TELEMACHUS
All right. So I get to Pylos. What next once I'm there?
CAPTAIN MENTES
Assemble the elders. Demand a big parley.
TELEMACHUS
Those old men love quarrelling. Bunch of rattling sticks.
CAPTAIN MENTES
The cord of your voice must bind those sticks together.
TELEMACHUS
I envy my father's authority.
CAPTAIN MENTES
Or tricks.
TELEMACHUS
Tricks?
CAPTAIN MENTES
I too saw the wooden horse blocking the stars.
(MELANTHO *exits.*)
EURYCLEIA
You see?
CAPTAIN MENTES
Troy fell for it.
TELEMACHUS
Was he that brilliant?

CAPTAIN MENTES
A horse foaling men? They thought it ridiculous.
EURYCLEIA
Him could convince a grasshopper it was a ant.
CAPTAIN MENTES
Look there! A swallow trying to get through the roof!
(*He exits.*)
EURYCLEIA
Me don't see it. Now where him gone? How that happen?
TELEMACHUS
He was Athena! Do you need any more proof?
EURYCLEIA
No.
TELEMACHUS
Then I'll follow the winged heels of my captain.
(*He exits.* PENELOPE *returns, attended by* MELANTHO,
who whispers in PENELOPE'*s ear.*)
PENELOPE
Who told you to stay so close to me, Melantho?
EURYCLEIA
Because Melantho have ambitions of her own.
MELANTHO
Ambitions?
EURYCLEIA
                    Madame, it have things that you don't know.
PENELOPE
You can have my sorrow, Melantho, with my throne.
MELANTHO
I don't want your throne, she's lying. Eurycleia!
PENELOPE
Look, girl, there are ways of putting your fire out.
EURYCLEIA
You didn't boast to me in the kitchen?
MELANTHO
                              Liar!

EURYCLEIA
That some prince in there go marry you?
MELANTHO
                              LIES!
PENELOPE
                                   DON'T SHOUT!
EURYCLEIA
Madame ...
PENELOPE
                    He left with this stranger? Are you crazy?
MELANTHO
Some shining young captain was here who fought at Troy.
PENELOPE
Stay in the kitchen.
MELANTHO
                        Not for long. Please excuse me.
(*She exits, brushing past* EURYCLEIA. *A burst of song from
the* SUITORS.)
EURYCLEIA
Madame, him is of age, him no longer a boy.
PENELOPE
The bloody war's over. Can't they sing something else?
EURYCLEIA
Him gone and pack him things.
PENELOPE
                              Pack his things? He's gone? Where?
EURYCLEIA
God, whatever we suffer we bring on we selves!
PENELOPE
Talk!
EURYCLEIA
        Some swallow talk to him, then it disappear.
PENELOPE
Swallow? Old woman, you want my palm on your face?
EURYCLEIA
Hit me, go on.

PENELOPE

        Why not tell me he was leaving?

(*She embraces* EURYCLEIA.)

EURYCLEIA

Melantho who tell you. She is always the first.

PENELOPE

Melantho helps me to unravel my weaving.

EURYCLEIA

True.

PENELOPE

      We fold his clothes in camphor. Unoccupied.

EURYCLEIA

So long in their press, them fit Telemachus now.

PENELOPE

I've knelt by our olive-tree bed, I've prayed and prayed.

EURYCLEIA

But him knew you would last.

PENELOPE

                How in hell could he know?

EURYCLEIA

Mistress, is strong-timbered virtues uphold this house.

PENELOPE

Till my patience cracks and it plunges in chaos.

EURYCLEIA

Because none in there can match the husband you choose.

PENELOPE

Yes, choose and then lose him. Who next? Telemachus?

(*She breaks down.* EUMAEUS *enters.*)

EURYCLEIA

Not now, Eumaeus, a family crisis here.

EUMAEUS

Since when am I excluded from this family?

EURYCLEIA

Back to the kitchen, old man.

EUMAEUS

           I brought the order.

PENELOPE
Eumaeus, listen! My one son has left this house.
EUMAEUS
Where's he gone, Mistress?
EURYCLEIA
                              Why you don't mind your business?
EUMAEUS
It's her business, fifty hogs and fifty prime sows.
EURYCLEIA
Go!
EUMAEUS
The stock's running out at a rate. Now this news.
PENELOPE
Eumaeus, you believe the Master's safe, don't you?
EUMAEUS
Safe? 'Fine day,' I thought, goading pigs up the white road.
PENELOPE
Say he's safe, Eumaeus. Now my son has gone, too.
EUMAEUS
Their trotters dancing. Happy at being slaughtered.
(EURYCLEIA *shows* EUMAEUS *out.*)
PENELOPE
He dotes on Odysseus. That's the weight he bears.
EURYCLEIA
Him old, but take good care of the stock all the same.
PENELOPE
They raced by rivers together, hunting wild boars.
EURYCLEIA
His ears does prick like the dog at Odysseus' name.
(ANTINOUS *enters.*)
ANTINOUS
Does your son believe he's the master of this house?
PENELOPE
He is. He's of age.
ANTINOUS
                              He shouted at your suitors.

EURYCLEIA
Dat is him right, sar! His father still Odysseus.

ANTINOUS
SHUT UP!
(*To* PENELOPE) See how a servant talks in front of us?

PENELOPE
She is this house's foundation. She was his nurse.

ANTINOUS
Well, her dugs are dry now.
(*To* EURYCLEIA)   Listen, you! No more noise!

PENELOPE
'If I die, marry,' he said, and sloped to his wars.

ANTINOUS
To lead an army of shadows. Death is his bride.

PENELOPE
When you prove my divorce, I'll follow his orders.

ANTINOUS
Ord-ysseus is lost since Troy, his wish disobeyed.

PENELOPE
You're the great pine above those suppliant princes.

ANTINOUS
You've made a hundred men think they're like no one else.

PENELOPE
You'll soon win your siege. I've run out of devices.

ANTINOUS
Then that wall is down that you built between ourselves?

PENELOPE
The wall has cracks in its face.

ANTINOUS
                              Bend that proud neck. Nod.

PENELOPE
A nod could be final.

ANTINOUS
                    Let one nod finish me.

PENELOPE
Another dead husband?

18

ANTINOUS

One nod is all I need.

PENELOPE

To die?

ANTINOUS

For one arrow from those eyes? Happily.

(MELANTHO *enters*.)

MELANTHO

Don't punish me, sir, but I have serious news.

ANTINOUS

Better make it good, girl, or I'll lop off that nose.

MELANTHO

The boy has gone.

EURYCLEIA

Melantho!

ANTINOUS

Gone? Telemachus?

MELANTHO

Look in the harbour. He stole your ship, Antinous.

PENELOPE

Poor girl! You were the last jewel left of my trust.

ANTINOUS

There was some sea captain here. You know who he was?

(*He grabs* EURYCLEIA.)

EURYCLEIA

Me no see no sea cap'n, sir! Leggo me wrist!

(ANTINOUS *releases* EURYCLEIA.)

MELANTHO

She's been unravelling the same shroud for three years.

ANTINOUS

Ah! I understand. Call in the others. Right now!

(MELANTHO *exits*.)

PENELOPE

You touch my son and you'll face my husband's revenge.

ANTINOUS

Your husband is dead. What sword can slice a shadow?

PENELOPE
    No!
ANTINOUS
        Let him return. He'll see how your patience ends.
PENELOPE
    My patience wasn't slavery, it was pure trust.
ANTINOUS
    And mine for three years. Get our marriage bed ready.
PENELOPE
    Look, sir, my vows aren't brooches I wear till they rust.
ANTINOUS
    Neither is my star, that's kept its distance, lady.
    (AMPHINOMUS *and* CTESIPPUS *enter, armed.*)
AMPHINOMUS
    The girl told us.
ANTINOUS
                        Arm two fast vessels!
CTESIPPUS
                                    There's no wind.
ANTINOUS
    If you lose him, hide in some cranny of the coast.
AMPHINOMUS
    Right!
ANTINOUS
                Post sentinels on the crags of each island.
AMPHINOMUS
    They'll roost till they turn into eagles, Antinous!
ANTINOUS
    Very odd! He's never acted this way before.
AMPHINOMUS
    Well, with this ambush he won't act this way after.
ANTINOUS
    He was simply sullen, until this visitor.
CTESIPPUS
    Then this island is ours. No more son, no father!
    (AMPHINOMUS *and* CTESIPPUS *exit.*)

ANTINOUS
If he dies your stubbornness put him in the earth.
PENELOPE
You think I'd step over his grave into your arms?
ANTINOUS
I'd rather not kill him. But if that's what you're worth.
PENELOPE
I'll bend when the bow bends.
ANTINOUS

What bow?
PENELOPE

The one that aims.
(*Points at his heart.*)
ANTINOUS
You're like some olive tree, waiting for her shadow.
PENELOPE
And you would wrench her last leaves: son, Eurycleia.
ANTINOUS
That hot blue sea stays empty. That sail you pine for.
PENELOPE
Its line is my bow-string, and its waves my lyre.
(ANTINOUS *exits.*)
EURYCLEIA
Me lost a husband too. Him was a damn scoundrel.
PENELOPE
Eurycleia!
EURYCLEIA

But me miss the scamp all the same.
PENELOPE
My hope is like a little lamp on a black hill.
EURYCLEIA
Yes, and when night coming down, is the worse, madam.
PENELOPE
Our bed is white and quiet. It's smooth with silence.
EURYCLEIA
Me know how linen keep still when somebody die.

PENELOPE
His shadow slides on my wall. I feel his presence.
EURYCLEIA
Oh, ma'am!
PENELOPE
I turn, and my glance makes his shadow fly.
(*They exit. Shadows of crossing oars, increasing speed.*
BILLY BLUE *enters.*)
CHORUS OF OARSMEN (*Chanting off*)
Ayis! Do-o! Trayis! Tetra! Pente! Ex!
Ayis! Do-o! Trayis! Tetra! Pente! Ex!
BILLY BLUE (*Sings*)
A one, a two, a three, four, five, six goes the mattock
Of the boatswain as the oarsmen bend their necks

Racing like mullet from the shadow of a sea-hawk.
Ayis! Do-o! Trayis! Tetra! Pente! Ex!

So mowers will increase the circle of their scythes,
Flailing at the waves of grass bowing from the wind

So the long blades of the rowers race for their lives
Towards Pylos, past Samos, leaving their hunters behind

Who spin back like sea-hawks, tired of the chase,
The oars fanned towards Pylos, then closed near Nestor's
palace.
(*Exits.*)

SCENE III

Nestor's palace. Interior. TELEMACHUS *and* CAPTAIN
MENTES *waiting.*

TELEMACHUS
You got here fast. Been to Temesa already?

CAPTAIN MENTES
A following wind.

TELEMACHUS
Struck a good deal with the bronze?

CAPTAIN MENTES
The bronze? Oh, the bronze! Let's say the wind was steady.

TELEMACHUS
Wasn't your cargo iron?

CAPTAIN MENTES
What's the difference?

TELEMACHUS
Athena . . .

CAPTAIN MENTES
Wait. Your hunters, what happened to them?

TELEMACHUS
They got tired like hawks. We cheered, watching them turn.

CAPTAIN MENTES
You had twenty great oarsmen.

TELEMACHUS
Like scythes in rhythm.

CAPTAIN MENTES
Those hawks will hover in inlets for your return.
(NESTOR *enters, with* ATTENDANTS.)

TELEMACHUS
Is this Nestor? That aged?

CAPTAIN MENTES
Surf-haired. He always was.

NESTOR
I cracked brine-seasoned whips over foaming horses.

CAPTAIN MENTES
Sir, Captain Mentes. This prince is Telemachus.

NESTOR
He enraged the sea, your father, Odysseus.

FIRST ATTENDANT
The sea's a maw that devours.

NESTOR

A god who saves.

TELEMACHUS

He saved you.

FIRST ATTENDANT

To his shame, image of Odysseus.

SECOND ATTENDANT

From Poseidon's charging herd, the unbridled waves.

NESTOR

No whip dipped in brine can steer the sea's white horses.

TELEMACHUS

The sea's ungovernable, is that what you mean?

NESTOR

Does he love questions? Another Odysseus!

TELEMACHUS

Sir . . .

NESTOR

Young Odysseus! You finish what I mean!

TELEMACHUS

Where's my father? Each dusk the sea-swallow steers home.

NESTOR

There's brilliance in here.

FIRST ATTENDANT

Your eyes, watering. The glare.

(NESTOR *peers at* MENTES.)

NESTOR

No. Like when your bright feet, Athena, skim the foam.

CAPTAIN MENTES

I'm Captain Mentes, sir.

NESTOR

No. The clouds' messenger.

CAPTAIN MENTES

When was that, sir?

NESTOR

At Troy. A swallow twittering.

24

TELEMACHUS
That was when you last saw my father. Is that right?

NESTOR
We looked up, unhelmeted, every blood-grimed king.

FIRST ATTENDANT
All of Troy's sorrow is borne in a swallow's flight.

NESTOR
Ten years! And my heart is stabbed by a bird's twitter.

CAPTAIN MENTES
Kites cried there, and ravens, the sky one black complaint.

NESTOR
Her voice was as close as yours.

CAPTAIN MENTES
                            Why, does it matter?

NESTOR
Yes. Athena was that swallow's inhabitant.

TELEMACHUS
In my small harbour harp songs ripple the water.

CAPTAIN MENTES
With heavy sadness.

TELEMACHUS
                        An anchor.

CAPTAIN MENTES
                            Troy's kings are home.

TELEMACHUS
Their feet are washed by servants. There's wine, and laughter.

CAPTAIN MENTES
His mother smooths the white sheets, then kneels there for
    him.

NESTOR
I crashed like a horse in surf, felled by exhaustion.

CAPTAIN MENTES
All the tired kings.

NESTOR
                    The bed heaving.

TELEMACHUS

                              Not my father.

FIRST ATTENDANT

You may have lost your father. But he's lost a son.

NESTOR

Oh, where's he, my shipmate? His ship! Cyclones toss it.

FIRST ATTENDANT

It'll turn up.

SECOND ATTENDANT

              Keel upward.

NESTOR

                        Our fleet melted in rain.

TELEMACHUS

Sir . . .

NESTOR

       That sea's so wide birds take a year to cross it.

TELEMACHUS

Nestor, I'm sorry that I cause you so much pain.

NESTOR

Odysseus' prow dolphined over black combers.

TELEMACHUS

Does he still remember every ornate detail?

FIRST ATTENDANT

His mind will cloud soon, and then he disremembers.

NESTOR

I watched the snail's silver of his diminished sail.

FIRST ATTENDANT

He scorned the sea, that is the last irreverence.

NESTOR

Your father reduced to reason every omen.

SECOND ATTENDANT

He defied the sea, where no force can pitch its tents.

NESTOR

Spray spat on great Agamemnon, that king of men.

SECOND ATTENDANT

Two silvery currents fork that sea. He turned left.

26

FIRST ATTENDANT
Your father turned right.
SECOND ATTENDANT
Apparently right was wrong.
NESTOR
It trembled on the world's rim, far from those he loved.
FIRST ATTENDANT
He's tired now. He shouldn't have spoken this long.
NESTOR
Across the ungirdered sea, the sky's foundation.
FIRST ATTENDANT
Where the sea-wall has measured its dividing line.
NESTOR
Through twisted pillars of rainspouts his bright wake shone.
CAPTAIN MENTES
Still, all of his old friends pray for his long return.
NESTOR
The ship crawled like a fly up the wall of the sea.
TELEMACHUS
And then?
SECOND ATTENDANT
Then, I suppose, it fell over the edge.
TELEMACHUS
And vanished, for good?
FIRST ATTENDANT
Or evil, evidently.
NESTOR
Through this world's pillars, the gate of human knowledge.
SECOND ATTENDANT
He's not the surf. He gets tired of his own speech.
NESTOR
The shame I feel for Odysseus, because I'm home.
TELEMACHUS
He would forgive you.
FIRST ATTENDANT
His mind's a sea-mist now. Come.

TELEMACHUS (*Aside to* MENTES)
What have I learned from this foam-haired philosopher?
CAPTAIN MENTES
What the young should learn. Patience.
TELEMACHUS
                                                        He's told me nothing.
CAPTAIN MENTES
You heard what the young need to hear: old men suffer.
TELEMACHUS
Don't disappear again, Captain. Where're you going?
(*The* CAPTAIN *exits.*)
NESTOR
                                                Give him a chariot. The finest.
TELEMACHUS
Bless you, Nestor.
SECOND ATTENDANT
                                Where's your friend?
NESTOR
                                                Blessings on your house.
FIRST ATTENDANT
Sit by your old blue window and watch the waves rust.
NESTOR
Gallop to Sparta and question Menelaus.
(*He is led off.* TELEMACHUS *mounts the chariot. Actors
mime two horses. They exit. Enter* BILLY BLUE.)
BILLY BLUE (*Sings*)
On the pebble road through undulant Lacedaemon,
Like a young Nestor, he urges the chariot on.

Then the horses rear, at the sight of another omen.
At the sight of another omen, the horses rear,

Nearly pitching the boy, who saw Athena's omen
As an eagle hurtled and snatched a trembling hare.

Then the horses raced their long shadows over again,
Huts lit their lamps on the hills and the ways darkened.

The sun fell down like a tower on Troy's black plain,
The stars' candles fluttered but didn't go out in the wind.

So haya! he cries, haya! to the frothing horses.
The starlight shines on their sweating flanks, their heads

Plunging like porpoises, until he saw the torches
From the palace of Menelaus, all the kings of Troy in their
    beds.
(*Exits.*)

SCENE IV

Sparta. Menelaus' palace. TELEMACHUS *kneels.*
MENELAUS *enters.*

TELEMACHUS
    I bring you Nestor's regards. He gave me his whip.
MENELAUS
    Ah, Nestor! How is Nestor? Great charioteer.
TELEMACHUS
    Tired.
MENELAUS
        Nestor. A foaming beard near a black ship.
TELEMACHUS
    He mourns his son.
MENELAUS
              I know. None knew our fates, back there.
TELEMACHUS
    But isn't home God's bounty, great Menelaus?
MENELAUS
    No. God's trial. We earn home, like everything else.
TELEMACHUS
    Still, you're back home, with your wife, in a great palace.

MENELAUS

All heaven's treasury cannot ransom my loss.

TELEMACHUS

What loss?

MENELAUS

They butchered my brother, Agamemnon.

TELEMACHUS

Who, sir?

MENELAUS

A cunning lover. A treacherous wife.

TELEMACHUS

Why?

MENELAUS

I leap up, drenched in cold sweat, I hear him moan.

TELEMACHUS

God!

MENELAUS

The net of his red veins fraying from the knife.

TELEMACHUS

Horrible.

MENELAUS

That enough fortune? For the jealous?

TELEMACHUS

No man should envy your wealth, poor Menelaus.

MENELAUS

Some heartless shadow stalks the House of Atreus.

TELEMACHUS

But love could frighten it, and sunlight flood your house.

MENELAUS

Yes. The cause and cloud of Troy will sail through that
  door.

(*Silence.* HELEN *enters.*)

HELEN

I'm Helen. Or I used to be. You're most welcome.

(*Silence.* TELEMACHUS *is staring.*)

TELEMACHUS
  I understand all. Sorry. You confirm a wonder.
HELEN
  Ohh . . .
MENELAUS
       Spears should surround her, not servants. But she's
         home.
HELEN
  I had no idea he had such a strapping boy.
MENELAUS
  Odysseus has spent ten years without coming home.
HELEN
  Well, at least he's travelling.
MENELAUS
                    She's bored. She misses Troy.
HELEN
  I do *not* miss Troy.
MENELAUS
              Miss being its centre. Its cause.
HELEN
  Don't I look quite happy to you?
MENELAUS
                     Think he'll say no?
HELEN
  'Miss Troy'! That's a stupid remark, Menelaus.
MENELAUS
  Sorry, dear.
HELEN
          Men. They'll blame me for everything now.
MENELAUS
  I don't think he came here to watch us bickering.
HELEN
  The whole thing was not over me but some sea-tax.
MENELAUS
  Oh? Your memory's fading like your hair dye, darling.

HELEN
Did I say I missed Troy? You and your cheap attacks.
(*She exits.*)
MENELAUS
She's a hard time sleeping. She remembers it all.
TELEMACHUS
There's an Egyptian herb that my mother uses.
MENELAUS
She leaps up. Torches on the water. The black wall.
TELEMACHUS
She caused much pain.
MENELAUS
                              Including yours for Odysseus.
TELEMACHUS
Do you think he's dead?
MENELAUS
                              Too smart. Too acquisitive.
TELEMACHUS
But did he ever take bounty he'd never earned?
MENELAUS (*Laughs*)
That sacker of cities? He'd say, 'Kings have to live.'
TELEMACHUS
He did well from the war?
MENELAUS
                              For him that's why Troy burned.
TELEMACHUS
Surely that wasn't all?
MENELAUS
                              It meant more than the war.
TELEMACHUS
Outright pillaging?
MENELAUS
                              Like the shield, he took his share.
TELEMACHUS
He sounds like a rug-seller, not a warrior.

MENELAUS
Oh, he's coming back well-loaded, you can be sure.
TELEMACHUS
What else?
MENELAUS
He loved to eat. Enormous appetite!
(*He laughs.*)
TELEMACHUS
What did he like?
MENELAUS
Like? Anything. Ate like a goat.
TELEMACHUS
I'm embarrassed.
MENELAUS
His motto was 'First eat, then fight.'
TELEMACHUS
What would you do?
MENELAUS
We'd eat. Even Ajax the Great.
(HELEN *enters, pushing a golden cart on silver wheels. She sits some distance off and weaves.* TELEMACHUS *rises.*)
MENELAUS
She'll sit there quietly. Nothing will distract her.
(*Silence.*)
She cracked the horizon's heart like any other.
(*Silence.*)
Now she's quiet marble, with light for her sculptor.
(*Silence.*)
Only the sea-breeze stirring the fringe of her hair.
(*Silence.*)
A flawed vase, now sealed, redeemed by its collector.
(*Silence.*)
One that sighs sometimes at the hollowness of war.
(*Silence.*)
But she's a good wife again. A perfect mother.
(*Turns to* TELEMACHUS.)

I know you're thinking, was all Troy's turmoil worth her?
(*Silence.*)
To bring her home? All that chaos? What's your answer?
TELEMACHUS
    It was.
MENELAUS
            I have a theory about your father.
HELEN
    The wool, please.
    (MENELAUS *picks up the wool, hands it to* HELEN.)
TELEMACHUS
                        Whatever helps twenty years of love.
HELEN
    Seals. Fog. And an old man, changing.
MENELAUS
                            Smile. You weren't there.
HELEN
    Show him the figured vase now.
MENELAUS
                        Watch this. He'll dissolve.
    (*A* SERVANT *enters with a vase, exits.*)
TELEMACHUS
    Your sail's way ahead of mine, sir.
HELEN
                            It always is.
TELEMACHUS
    I see fog. An old man, creeping. What does it mean?
HELEN
    Forgive me your pain, image of Odysseus.
TELEMACHUS
    I do.
    (HELEN *exits.*)
MENELAUS
    Look, the wine-dark sea, veined aquamarine.
TELEMACHUS
    Go on.

MENELAUS
        Can you knot the mist? Cup fog in your hand?
TELEMACHUS
    And this figure sprang from the sea in different shapes?
MENELAUS
    He scuttled crab-wise from the surf, burrowing in sand.
TELEMACHUS
    Who is he?
MENELAUS
            Proteus. He's fluent. He escapes.
TELEMACHUS
    This is my old nurse's tale, great Menelaus.
MENELAUS
    Then consider yourself forever in her debt.
TELEMACHUS
    Why?
MENELAUS
        The gates of imagination never close.
TELEMACHUS
    Even in grown men?
MENELAUS
                What are men? Children who doubt.
TELEMACHUS
    Go on.
MENELAUS
        Dawn. The Nile's mouth, exhaling. Barking seals.
    (Seals bark. Fog.)
TELEMACHUS (Points)
    Your ship?
MENELAUS
            Blown months off course by a remorseless wind.
TELEMACHUS
    Then, through fog, this crawls?
MENELAUS
                    Net-slinger, he catches souls.

TELEMACHUS
You think he's caught my father's?
MENELAUS

                                  It has crossed my mind.
TELEMACHUS
Men aren't crabs, Menelaus.
MENELAUS

                                    We hid in seal-skins.
TELEMACHUS
My father is alive, alive. He's lost, that's all.
MENELAUS
That crooked old man. I wrestled him with questions.
TELEMACHUS
Like what, sir?
MENELAUS

                          Under stinking seal-skins. We kept still.
TELEMACHUS
While the fog shaped these? A snake, a cloudy lion?
MENELAUS
Shh. Creeping. A crab. Sand-wise. Testing the foam.
TELEMACHUS
Oh, I see him! Through that net of spray. What question?
MENELAUS
What my prayers urged me. The soul's question. Which
    way home?
(PROTEUS *appears.* ODYSSEUS *appears. He wrestles with*
PROTEUS *in the fog.* PROTEUS *points.* ODYSSEUS *follows*
his direction. MENELAUS *exits.* TELEMACHUS *sits alone.*
Torches go out. The vase begins to whirl, with the loud
sound of water. TELEMACHUS *rises, walks down to the*
morning beach.)
TELEMACHUS
ECHO ME, ISLANDS! ODYS-SEUS! ODYSEE...
ECHO

                      SEA, SEA, SEA... ODYSEEEE...

TELEMACHUS
  I WANT TO SEE YOU, FATHER!
ECHO
                                        FARTHER,
                                          FARTHER...
TELEMACHUS
  CARRY MY CRY THROUGH YOUR CAVES!
ECHO
                                             CAVES!
TELEMACHUS
  PAST VOLISSOS, CHIOS, DELOS, ITHACA...
ECHO
                                              CARE!
  (TELEMACHUS *sits on the sand.*)
TELEMACHUS
  Help him to wrestle the weed-bearded waves...
  (*Surf, sibilance.* TELEMACHUS *exits.*)

                    SCENE V

  Odysseus' ship, being loaded. SAILORS STRATIS, COSTA,
  STAVROS *and* TASSO *chanting.*

SAILORS
  Get a load of this, boys, handle with care
  Gifts our cap'n's bringing home from Troy to Ithaca.

  Bales from cities that he sacked on his way home,
  Gifts from King Aeolus, maybe he'll spare some.
STAVROS
  In my mountains, snow. March dreaming of October.
COSTA
  It's mis'rible there. The mountains. Pissing with rain.
TASSO
  Who's warming the wife, Stavros? Ramming it to her?

                    37

(STAVROS *draws a knife. A scuffle.* STRATIS *intervenes.*)
STAVROS
  My wife good woman.
STRATIS
                    Save the knife for our captain.
  (*He takes the knife. Loading continues.*)
STAVROS
  Wonder what stories our captain pitched to the king?
COSTA
  Enough for these gifts to weigh down her water line.
TASSO
  Done all right by the war, din't he? Looting, sacking.
COSTA
  That's why he's 'Sacker of Cities'. You'll never learn.
TASSO
  Bounty from Troy! See that, Stavros? Widen your eyes.
STRATIS
  What's your salary? Salt. Live off that forever!
  (*A huge bag is shipped aboard.*)
COSTA
  Here's that bag the king gave Captain Odysseus.
TASSO
  Aeolus rules this island but not its weather.
STRATIS
  He wants to get home, but stops off to plunder cities?
COSTA
  Leaving their coasts smoking with his anger. The Great!
TASSO
  Just like you, shepherd, he has faith in his missis.
COSTA
  He's making sure old age isn't singed with regret.
  (*They stow the bag.*

  Upper deck. They're under way. ODYSSEUS *hangs the
  shield on the mast.* ELPENOR *is at the helm.*)

ODYSSEUS
Steer. Elpenor, I've forgotten, how old are you?

ELPENOR
Another quarter moon, sir, I'll be twenty-two.

ODYSSEUS
Twenty-two! My son's age. Or, rather, half a son.

ELPENOR
Why half a son, sir?

ODYSSEUS
                His other half could be you.

ELPENOR
The croak of that mast. Like a crow, crossing a field.

ODYSSEUS
A tower cracking. Troy, Troy! What was it all worth?

ELPENOR
Not a crow. More like a sheep that strayed from the fold.

ODYSSEUS
I'd give up all this heaving for one yard of earth.

ELPENOR
You'll soon see the sunlight wet those homecoming oars.

ODYSSEUS
Even monsters on the bottom crawl to their bed.

ELPENOR
You're as lucky as they are, sir. You're close to yours.

ODYSSEUS
Islands weary me now. Foam is flecking this head.

ELPENOR
A clean white bed is all a man asks for on earth.
(ODYSSEUS *taps the mast.*)

ODYSSEUS
I think of that olive tree my bed was made from.

ELPENOR
Aye, sir.

ODYSSEUS
           And those stars flying. Embers from my hearth.

ELPENOR
   Captain?
ODYSSEUS
               No night was so long. No dawn more welcome.
ELPENOR
   No.

(*Below deck.*)
STRATIS
   Once, it was off Smyrna, I cut a captain's throat.
TASSO
   Like a sheep.
STRATIS
               Right, he bored me. Kept bleating of home.
TASSO
   That's his drift, isn't it?
STRATIS
               Home's just another threat.
COSTA
   So you're stuck with killers of sheep, shepherd. Welcome.
   (ODYSSEUS *descends from the upper deck with a lantern,*
   tours the crew. Boatswain's mattock is beating.)
ODYSSEUS
   By dawn's edge, Ithaca. By star-rise, my own roof.
STRATIS
   Been how many seasons since you left home, Captain?
ODYSSEUS
   Twenty. The sea air smells friendlier.
STRATIS
                           Could get rough.
ODYSSEUS
   When sunrise comes, I'll give the dawn back her lantern.
COSTA
   'Home'! The word that a gull cries over wild waters.
ODYSSEUS
   I've a boy I haven't seen for half of my life.

TASSO

They've shot up like pliant saplings, my two daughters.

STRATIS

For me, home is a breathing death. Back to the wife.
(*Laughter.*)

ODYSSEUS

These oars multiply the image of what we love.

TASSO

For me, home is grey fields with a ploughman's fire.

COSTA

Sometimes it's a smell. I'm pierced by the scent of clove.

TASSO

A grime-streaked angel gesturing from its spire.

STRATIS

For me, Captain, a reef in the battering surf.

COSTA

Objects outlast us. Spice tins on a kitchen shelf.

STRATIS

Until he enters his own grave, sir, no man is safe.

ODYSSEUS

Then call me 'No-man', but your friendship is my wealth.
(*He climbs back up to the upper deck.*)

STRATIS

What've you got from the sea? A fistful of silver.

COSTA

Or a school of flying fish, scattering like stars.

STRATIS

That's the sum of it. You live off that forever.

TASSO

That bag Aeolus gave him. Whatever it was.

STRATIS

He'll be up on that deck for a while. Where's the bag?

COSTA

He stuffed it under his bunk.

STAVROS

                              Will he be killed?

STRATIS
He's made his fortune, Stavros. No sharing the swag.
TASSO
He's made a pile from the war. Gold cups, coins, that shield.
STRATIS
I'm going down. Tap three times if he comes.

(*Upper deck.*)
ODYSSEUS
Oh, the kings I've known, who saw themselves as fixed stars!
ELPENOR
What kings, sir?
ODYSSEUS
    My far comrades at Troy.
ELPENOR
            But their fame?
ODYSSEUS
They were meteors, in their long fall from greatness.
ELPENOR
Why?
ODYSSEUS
  That sea simplifies them, Elpenor. To foam.
(*He is peeing over the side.*)
ELPENOR
How can you keep your balance, without tumbling off?
ODYSSEUS
Feet braced. I'm steady, helmsman. It's those stars that aren't.
ELPENOR
They're swaying like scales. Can you do that when it's rough?
ODYSSEUS
Stars! Look! the sprinkled urine of the firmament!
ELPENOR
Day will break soon. A dawn breeze soothing the mind.
ODYSSEUS
Those waves are leaves in my garden . . .

ELPENOR
                              Sounds a nice place.
ODYSSEUS
  And on the lawn over which a hunched oak towers.
ELPENOR
  Would you care to sit down, Captain? I'll make some space.
ODYSSEUS
  My stone bench anchored in a foam of white flowers.
  (*Lightning.*)
ELPENOR
  There, sir, through that crack of light on the horizon!
ODYSSEUS
  They're just the distant flashes of a summer storm.
ELPENOR
  Wait now, sir! Where pronged lightning forks the sea's
  garden?
ODYSSEUS
  What, boy?
ELPENOR
                  You knelt there, pruning flower beds of foam.
ODYSSEUS
  Your watch ends when?
ELPENOR
                              Sunrise, sir.
ODYSSEUS
                              I'll believe you if . . .
ELPENOR
  If what, sir?
ODYSSEUS
                  If you'll admit to wine on your breath.
ELPENOR
  Well, me and the crew had a jar earlier, sir.
ODYSSEUS
  Steer carefully. A cloud can harden to a cliff.

  (*Below deck.*)

COSTA
  Open the knot.
STRATIS
                There's nothing in there, just wind.
TASSO
  You're lying.
STAVROS
                It's getting dark suddenly, why?
TASSO
  Get up and look again, clod! Up, under, behind!
COSTA
  What's that noise? It's like windmills churning up the sky?
ODYSSEUS
  They've opened the bag. Now the seas are mountainous.
ELPENOR
  Look! White sheep scattering from the fork of that storm!
ODYSSEUS
  Something has injured this sea. It's breaking our oars.
  (*Sound of breaking oars.*)
COSTA
  They're cracking like bones in a dog's teeth.
ODYSSEUS (*To* ELPENOR)
                WATCH THAT STERN!
ELPENOR
  There's sunrise. Ithaca! A pink cloud and mountain!
  (*Sunrise.*)
ODYSSEUS
                HARD WITH THAT HELM!
STRATIS
  Ay! The blue's turning greener where shallows begin.
ELPENOR
  ITHACA, CAPTAIN! LET'S KNEEL DOWN ON
  DECK! YOU'RE HOME!
ODYSSEUS
  THE HELM, DAMN YOU, BOY! Seagulls, the first
  fishermen.

(The ship lists sharply.)

COSTA

The island is tilting and that white mountain town.

ELPENOR

THE GULLS ARE THROWING THEIR CAPS IN THE
  AIR, CAPTAIN!

ODYSSEUS

HOLD ON TO THE BLOODY HELM, BOY, OR
  WE'LL ALL DROWN!

STRATIS

Where is it, Skipper?

ODYSSEUS

     Home! Poplars! Mount Neriton!

(ELPENOR is swept overboard.)

COSTA

HELMSMAN OVERBOARD, CAPTAIN!

ODYSSEUS

     Where's Achilles' shield? Gone?

FIRST SAILOR

CAPTAIN, THAT WAS THE HELMSMAN!

ODYSSEUS

    WE'RE BLOWING OFF COURSE!

STAVROS

You unknotted this wind! We are gone forever.

COSTA

We're lost sheep, Stavros.

ODYSSEUS

    ELPENOR! TELEMACHUS!

(The ship founders. All hands swept overboard.)

SCENE VI

*Cries, gulls or girls playing. A ball bounces across the sand. A
girl,* ANEMONE, *chases it out of sight. A screech.* ANEMONE
runs back to join NAUSICAA *and another girl,* CHLOE.

45

ANEMONE
　　I seen him, I seen him, the Old Man of the Sea!
NAUSICAA
　　Oh, girl, speak properly, and run back for my ball!
ANEMONE
　　Face down embracing the surf; please, please, believe me.
NAUSICAA
　　You saw a log with arms, don't get hysterical.
ANEMONE
　　I'm not hysterical!
CHLOE
　　　　　　　　I'll bet he was naked.
NAUSICAA
　　Why do you always ruin our games with nonsense?
ANEMONE
　　Beg pardon, Princess.
CHLOE
　　　　　　　　She's just got men in her head.
NAUSICAA
　　That's all you saw, girl. The dream of your secret sins.
ANEMONE
　　He was spraggled face down like a starfish! Naked!
CHLOE
　　Maybe a starfish is the Old Man of the Sea.
NAUSICAA
　　Or an octopus now, playing ball with eight hands.
ANEMONE
　　Why don't you fetch the ball, if you don't believe me?
CHLOE
　　'Cause she didn't throw it!
ANEMONE
　　　　　　　　A starfish! Without no pants!
(ODYSSEUS *appears, torn, naked, carrying the ball. The
two girls scream and run.* ODYSSEUS *throws the ball,
collapses.*)

NAUSICAA
Please get up, sir, don't lie on my kingdom naked.
ODYSSEUS
The sea has beaten me. My sight's not too clear.
NAUSICAA
You should put something on. This is very awkward.
ODYSSEUS
White cries rose behind these rocks. A wave rolled me here.
NAUSICAA
Oh, did the reef tear you? What happened to that arm?
ODYSSEUS
I was spun like driftwood by those smoking breakers.
NAUSICAA
That's the white, wild side of the island. Here it's calm.
ODYSSEUS
I woke to hear seagulls crying. They were girls' cries.
NAUSICAA
There was a wild storm last night, the oaks were groaning.
ODYSSEUS
I survived it. Swinging from a branch like a bat.
NAUSICAA
Still, after hurricanes there's the light of morning.
ODYSSEUS
Upside down, over the surf. Hearing the storm beat.
NAUSICAA
That's rough.
ODYSSEUS
                    O Nymph, whose freshness is sheer perfection!
NAUSICAA
Sheer? You'll gain nothing addressing me in that way.
ODYSSEUS
I am dazzled. My salt eyes are scorched by the sun.
NAUSICAA
That's how all these overtures start. With poetry.
ODYSSEUS
What poetry?

NAUSICAA
You know. 'O Nymph', and all that business.
ODYSSEUS
I thought I drowned and soared with the gulls to heaven.
NAUSICAA
See? Next you'll croak about clutching my shining knees.
ODYSSEUS
I will?
NAUSICAA
Why not just say it?
(*Pause.*)
Or think it, even?
ODYSSEUS
No.
NAUSICAA
Or talk about my eyes, like sea-green shallows.
ODYSSEUS
Yes. They are. You're right.
NAUSICAA
Or the pink shells of my ears?
ODYSSEUS
Nymph, I'll say no more than my nakedness allows.
NAUSICAA
Why?
ODYSSEUS
Because there's a huge gulf between us, girl. *Years!*
NAUSICAA
Don't bark at me like some seal! You know what you are?
ODYSSEUS
No.
NAUSICAA
A snarling, whiskered seal sunning on some reef.
(*She mimics a seal.*)
ODYSSEUS
Oh, am I?

NAUSICAA
       Blaming me for your catastrophe.

ODYSSEUS
You're well on your way to being somebody's wife.

NAUSICAA
Yours?

ODYSSEUS
     No. I'm too old. Plus, I have one already.

NAUSICAA
Too old, with that panelled body? Old is like this.
(*Crouches, clutching her back.*)

ODYSSEUS
You're an old man's delight.

NAUSICAA
              Shall we meet properly?

ODYSSEUS
Shall we?

NAUSICAA
     Nausicaa. And you're my gift from the seas!
(*She kisses his cheek. A roar.*)

ODYSSEUS
What's that noise in the throat of those hills?

NAUSICAA
                  Oh. The games.

ODYSSEUS
The games? What games?

NAUSICAA
        You'll see. When I get you some clothes.

ODYSSEUS
I've heard that cheering echo. Spears, hoisting dead names.

NAUSICAA
You're in tears.

ODYSSEUS
     More salt. For Elpenor. Troy's heroes.
(*He stops. Listens.*)

NAUSICAA
Were you a hero, too? Why are you stopping? Move.

ODYSSEUS
Every fuming breaker brings echoes of that war.

NAUSICAA
What war?

ODYSSEUS
                    Exactly.

NAUSICAA
                            It took you from those you love?

ODYSSEUS
Twenty years now.

NAUSICAA
                            Come. You'll tell it to my father.

(*They climb.*)

ODYSSEUS
Who's he, your father?

NAUSICAA
                            He's the king of this place.

ODYSSEUS
I lost ship, crew, a shield. I have nothing left.

NAUSICAA
We'll find them, I promise. I'm a real princess.

ODYSSEUS
I could tell.

NAUSICAA
            Liar.

ODYSSEUS
                    I could. From the way you laughed.

(ANEMONE *and* CHLOE *peer out, stop, advance.*
ODYSSEUS *walks ahead of* NAUSICAA.)

NAUSICAA
The map of the world's on your back. The skin's peeling.

ODYSSEUS
Sun and salt. For ten long years. What are your friends'
    names?

NAUSICAA
   Girls. This is Scheria, an isle known for healing.
ODYSSEUS
   By three gracious spirits.
NAUSICAA
                        And famous for its games.
   (*Distant cheering, louder. They exit.*)

                        SCENE VII

   Alcinous' palace. ATHLETES *and* COURTIERS *exercising.*
   Music. Trumpets. Cheering. ALCINOUS *steps on to a*
   platform. Drums and horns. BILLY BLUE *as* PHEMIUS.

BILLY BLUE (*Sings*)
   Fleet the bare feet of runners racing on the sand!
   Their ankles whirr like hummingbirds towards the laurel.

   Extending their arms like swallows as they reach the end,
   Their thighs are blurred ovals passing breakers of coral.

   What greater glory than what men win on their feet,
   Outdistancing friendly shadows in their short sun?

   Greater than poetry is the metre of the athlete
   Since their glory is brief, and swifter than any song.

   They turn into birds, they are stretching to leave the earth,
   They're pliant as otters, their heads sleek from the surf.

   But let them stay green as the Olympian laurel
   In the kindest of wars, the games, man's happiest quarrel.

   Kindle the torch, begin these Phaeacian games,
   Then, on plaques of gold, silver and bronze incise their names.
ALCINOUS
   First let us honour this shipwrecked stranger, our guest.
   (*Roar.*)

                        51

ODYSSEUS

Thanks, gentle Scherians. I'm enjoying it here.

ALCINOUS

In a while the games. He has accepted our test.

(*Laughter. Some booing.*)

ODYSSEUS

Well, I'm a bit rusty. You've every right to jeer.

(SECOND COURTIER *enters the ring. Takes javelin, hurls it out of sight.*)

FIRST COURTIER

That could nail an eagle. Out o' sight, man, out o' sight!

SECOND COURTIER

Here comes the runt now, he's shorter than the spear.

FIRST COURTIER

Bet you he puts out the sun's eye, turns day to night.

SECOND COURTIER

Bet you it drops like a swallow, tired of air.

(ODYSSEUS *hurls his javelin farther.*)

THIRD COURTIER

Knock me down with a feather! That's gone to Egypt!

FOURTH COURTIER

Send an expedition to find it. Heard that hum?

FIRST COURTIER

It sang like a swallow, man!

SECOND COURTIER

He's lucky. It slipped.

FOURTH COURTIER

Yeah? You slip over to Egypt and bring it home.

(ODYSSEUS *confronts a* YOUNG ATHLETE. ODYSSEUS *and the* YOUNG ATHLETE *wrestle.* ODYSSEUS *lets himself be thrown.*)

ODYSSEUS

I stopped because I imagined you were my son.

YOUNG ATHLETE

That's a good one, I never heard that one before.

ODYSSEUS
    I couldn't hurt you.
YOUNG ATHLETE
                    Try, you have my permission.
    (ODYSSEUS *throws him, pins him.*)
ODYSSEUS
    I keep seeing him. Telemachus. Elpenor.
    (*Cheering.* ALCINOUS *calls for silence.*)
    You see here a man who's lost all his worldly goods.
    (*General groan of sympathy.*)
    Who the sea-god hates, but who's survived every storm.
    (*Applause.*)
    Like a boar dodging the lightning-lances of gods.
    (*Imitates a boar. Laughter.*)
    A wanderer who knows your bounty will help him home.
    (*Silence.*)
    If you were simple men, I would tell you such things . . .
FOURTH COURTIER
    We live on islands. We might believe them, try us.
ODYSSEUS
    You are polished, sceptical men. My wanderings . . .
FIFTH COURTIER
    Yes?
ODYSSEUS
        Men used to hearing the surf curl in their ears.
ALCINOUS
    The more outlandish your tales, the more they'll please us.
NAUSICAA
    My father loves stories, he rewards their singers.
ODYSSEUS
    Devious Odysseus, divisive Odysseus.
SECOND COURTIER
    Did you know him?
ODYSSEUS
                    In Troy, that's what he was known as.

53

ALCINOUS
Troy's wind has touched every island with its ashes.
FIRST COURTIER
You'll do well singing about him, eh, Phemius?
NAUSICAA
You know his stories?
ODYSSEUS
That liar Odysseus?
SECOND COURTIER
Tell us his stories, stranger.
ODYSSEUS
In a sailor's prose?
THIRD COURTIER
As blind as he is, he'll stitch them into one song.
FIRST COURTIER
His lines can hum like a succession of arrows.
SECOND COURTIER
Or combers that crest from the shale, horizon-long.
FIRST COURTIER
They are like huge oars lifting, the heft of his lines.
THIRD COURTIER
Thudding like lances on to the heart of this earth.
SECOND COURTIER
He baffles augurs. He can hear the bird's designs.
FIRST COURTIER
He can smell the smoke of Troy, and that's far enough.
ALCINOUS
He can feel the truth. The way blind men sense the wind.
PHEMIUS
What lasts is what's crooked. The devious man survives.
ALCINOUS
Why'd you say that, Phemius? Because you're blind?
PHEMIUS
That's the way with tears. Crooked streams join their
    rivers.

ALCINOUS
Why has it taken so long to reach your kingdom?
NAUSICAA
You've found no mercy from the sea, make this your shore.
ODYSSEUS
No wanderer ever had a warmer welcome.
NAUSICAA
Tell us his enchantments.
ODYSSEUS
You've heard of Calypso?
LISTENERS
Yes.
ODYSSEUS
Her marble arms entombed him for seven years.
NAUSICAA
What kind of a woman was she? I know. Soft, but stern.
ODYSSEUS
Odysseus couldn't recognize Odysseus.
NAUSICAA
Most women who look like statues have hearts of stone.
ODYSSEUS
Foam girdles the waist of her island with white lace.
FIRST COURTIER
Nausicaa's blushing, look.
NAUSICAA
I'm not. Don't stop for me.
ALCINOUS
She's Atlas' daughter. What do they call the place?
ODYSSEUS
Like her dimpled white mound: the Navel of the Sea.
ALCINOUS
Return us to her island. Now that you're healing.
ODYSSEUS
A cave's blue entrance: alabaster, porphyry.
NAUSICAA
I'm sealing my eyes.

ODYSSEUS

Waves of light on its ceiling.

NAUSICAA

I hear a spring chuckling like a woman, softly.

ALCINOUS

You're too young for all of this, you've imagined enough.

ODYSSEUS

No, let her learn not to exploit her innocence.

NAUSICAA

Two bodies tangled in linen as white as surf.

ODYSSEUS

O Nymph, let your freshness salt and cure all my sins!

ALCINOUS

Was enchantment hidden in the island itself?

ODYSSEUS

In her and the island. One cleft of flesh, one of stone.

NAUSICAA

Soon I'll have the power to make grown men dissolve.

ALCINOUS (*To* NAUSICAA)

Girl!

(*To* ODYSSEUS)

They claim she tames fierce creatures, not men alone.

ODYSSEUS

Lions purr under her palm, wolves flatten their ears.

ALCINOUS

And those wild beasts prowled the door of light from her
cave?

ODYSSEUS

They growled when thoughts of home clouded Odysseus.

FIRST COURTIER

But didn't he find delight in her happy grave?

ODYSSEUS

No. He sank into a sadness no flesh could cure.

FIRST COURTIER

Sadness?

ODYSSEUS
        Longing for his island. She heard him weep.

NAUSICAA
Even while she oiled his body and brushed his hair?

ODYSSEUS
Leopards with lantern-eyes guarded their sleep.

NAUSICAA
Now she adores a mortal. Unhappy goddess!

ODYSSEUS
So she helps him build a tree-raft, fastened with vines.

NAUSICAA
He leaves?

ODYSSEUS
        He leaves one dawn, when clouds open their doors.

PHEMIUS
Our bodies long for their far shore, this raft of veins.

ALCINOUS
Yet he stayed there, cloud-pillowed, for seven years her
    guest.

FIRST COURTIER
How could a mere mortal break from immortal arms?

ODYSSEUS
Because that beach was shadowed by another's ghost.

FIRST COURTIER
Whose?

ODYSSEUS
        His wife's. The raft is ready. That moment comes.
    (*Silence.*)

ALCINOUS
Now?

ODYSSEUS
        The goddess offers godhead. He refuses.

FIRST COURTIER
He declines immortality? God! Tell us why!

ODYSSEUS
He longs for his own rock, too stony for horses.

FIRST COURTIER
    Over heaven?
ODYSSEUS
            It seemed natural. Men love, then die.
FIRST COURTIER
    But his name, Odysseus, rivetted in stars!
ODYSSEUS
    He prefers to kindle the lamps of his own house.
PHEMIUS
    And that house will be the lamp by which his raft steers.
NAUSICAA
    Monsters, more monsters! Let's have monster stories.
ODYSSEUS
    You beg for what he'd rather forget. Well. Monsters.
ALCINOUS
    Tonight you'll curl in clean linen, the shell of sleep.
NAUSICAA
    You'll smell rain in the earth, and when the hillsides shine
ALCINOUS
    You'll see purple vineyards laddering every slope.
NAUSICAA
    Then, our marriage-cart, drawn by nodding white oxen.
ODYSSEUS (*Laughing*)
    Whoa! Whoa! Not so fast! You deserve a good husband.
NAUSICAA
    There's a 'but'?
ODYSSEUS
            How'll I explain it to my wife?
    (*Laughter.*)
NAUSICAA
    Tell her you met me and were swept overboard and . . .
ODYSSEUS
    That's true.
NAUSICAA
            Wouldn't she be happy that I saved your life?

ALCINOUS
She's a smart girl but a bit too fresh for her age.
NAUSICAA
Goddesses can be so vulgar! Caves made of gems!
ALCINOUS (*To* PHEMIUS)
Listen, poet, and let your eyes seal each image.
NAUSICAA
Remember you heard them at the Phaeacian games.
ODYSSEUS
Sir, the truths I will tell are too full of horrors.
NAUSICAA
We idle in the sun. We never have nightmares.
ALCINOUS
Let's all move to another room to hear these stories.
ODYSSEUS
Some might redden the innocent shells of her ears.
NAUSICAA
Oh, please, please, begin your stories! You've a lot to gain.
ODYSSEUS
Then imagine an iron island. Sunless. Cold.
NAUSICAA
I'm shivering.
ODYSSEUS
          The future is where we begin.
NAUSICAA
Is this just a dream?
ODYSSEUS
          No. A place where dreams are killed.
(*All exit, except* BILLY BLUE, *still as* PHEMIUS, *and three*
COURTIERS.)
FIRST COURTIER
You can build a heavy-beamed poem out of this.
SECOND COURTIER
It will ride time to unknown archipelagoes.
PHEMIUS
I heard that voice at Troy. This is Odysseus.

THIRD COURTIER
　　Why lie about it? Natural cunning, I suppose.
　　(*They exit.*)
MARTIAL CHORUS (*Off*)
　　To die for the eye is best, it's the greatest glory:
　　Dulce et decorum est pro patria mori.

　　There is no I after the eye, no more history,
　　Except his own, Odysseus. This was his first story:

　　A sea, like lead, heavy as time's weight in water,
　　And a sullen harbour, eternally overcast.

　　Not a seabird beating, a thousand years in the future,
　　Time, altering the bodies where they were encased.

SCENE VIII

*A long, grey, empty wharf. A sheep's carcass, gutted,
hanging from a pole. An oil drum rolls on, chased by the*
PHILOSOPHER, *who rummages in the contents of the*
drum. ODYSSEUS, EURYLOCHUS *and two* SAILORS *enter.*

EURYLOCHUS
　　This is frightening, sir. What kind of city is this?
FIRST SAILOR
　　Like one long Sabbath, an infinite, empty wharf.
　　(*The* PHILOSOPHER *runs towards them.*)
PHILOSOPHER
　　History's repeated! A second Odysseus!
ODYSSEUS
　　Stop!
PHILOSOPHER
　　　　Wanderer, you'll need advice.
FIRST SAILOR
　　　　　　　　　　　　Listen, buzz off!

60

PHILOSOPHER
 They praised you once, Odysseus, forbidden phantom!
ODYSSEUS
 Sir, none of my virtues is nobler than all men's.
PHILOSOPHER
 Well, now you hear to what quiet a country can come.
EURYLOCHUS
 Apart from this bleating of sheep herded in pens.
FIRST SAILOR
 Sir, everywhere there's the sign of this giant eye!
PHILOSOPHER
 A man becomes nothing at that Zero's bidding.
ODYSSEUS
 Is this the Greece that I loved? Is this my city?
PHILOSOPHER
 Philosophy's cradle, where Thought is forbidden.
ODYSSEUS
 Can I see the Eye?
PHILOSOPHER
                    No, rather the Eye sees us.
EURYLOCHUS
 The Eye's their shepherd, and the nation are his sheep?
PHILOSOPHER
 Return to that age of heroes, Odysseus!
ODYSSEUS
 I'd like to see this monster. Does it ever weep?
PHILOSOPHER
 No.
ODYSSEUS
 And the wall?
PHILOSOPHER
                    Erected to keep us in pens.
ODYSSEUS
 So this city is nothing but a giant cave?
PHILOSOPHER
 With History erased, there's just the present tense.

ODYSSEUS
I breach walls.
PHILOSOPHER
For a freedom that men dare not crave?
(*Distant sound of a parade over the roofs of the city. Sings along.*)
Listen.
What to the eye is best, the greatest glory?
Dulce et decorum est – to die for a lie with zest –
Pro patria mori.
EURYLOCHUS
There is no art, no theatre, no circuses even?
PHILOSOPHER
This is the era of the grey colonels. Grey rain.
EURYLOCHUS
So one cold eye is all these Greeks know of heaven?
PHILOSOPHER
Their statues weep with grime over history's ruin.
ODYSSEUS
EURYLOCHUS, SHAKE ME! WAKE ME UP FROM
THIS DREAM!
(*Sound of a huge door closing.*)
EURYLOCHUS
The cave is blocked. We can't leave, Captain Odysseus.
PHILOSOPHER
The future happens. No matter how much we scream.
(*Sound of boots over cobbles, two* PATROLMEN *in sheepskin coats enter, carrying chains.*)
FIRST SAILOR
The Eye has found us.
PHILOSOPHER
Bay! Obey! Do what it says.
FIRST PATROLMAN
Do not talk to this one. He has slandered the Eye.
PHILOSOPHER
My turn has come.

SECOND PATROLMAN
                    By the way, what is your name, sir?
(*The* PHILOSOPHER *is seized.*)
PHILOSOPHER
  My name is Socrates Aristotle Lucretius. Philosopher.
  (*He is marched up against a wall, clubbed, then held
  upright.*)
FIRST PATROLMAN
  Lower your heads, you sheep! The Great Shepherd is here.
  (*The door opens and the* CYCLOPS *slowly approaches.
  Sound of cheering crowds, distantly.*)
PHILOSOPHER (*Recites*)
  Yet I was one among many thousands in the square,
  But always too late, too far at the back to see

  The smiles of the tiny faces on the balcony.
  Those in front with the caps, braids and medals, and those
      at the rear

  In coats and identical hats who didn't wave
  Like the central one, turning both profiles repeatedly

  Into a coin or a postage stamp. I had to be there
  With the roaring victims who craned or held up children

  And yelped and jumped high like dogs that you are training
  In that boxed, crammed square that felt like a mass grave

  To a drifting smell of formaldehyde or adrenaline,
  Learn what I remember, that someday it could save.

  But I swear, on my grave, now that it's all over,
  And the square and the balcony empty, I was there, but I
      didn't wave.
  (*The* PATROLMEN *remove him.*)
  Let the Greeks remember Odysseus the Brave!
  (*The* CYCLOPS *faces* ODYSSEUS.)

CYCLOPS
Don't stare.
ODYSSEUS
Sorry.
CYCLOPS
What is your name?
ODYSSEUS
Nobody.
CYCLOPS
Where're you from?
ODYSSEUS
Nowhere.
CYCLOPS (*Nodding*)
Where're you going?
ODYSSEUS
I don't know.
CYCLOPS
Nobody.
From nowhere.
Going where he doesn't know.
Normal.
No?
ODYSSEUS
Yes.
CYCLOPS
What do you believe in?
ODYSSEUS
Nothing. For now.
CYCLOPS
Nothing?
Not the Great Eye?
ODYSSEUS
Not yet.
CYCLOPS (*Laughing*)
Not yet?
Nyet.

Why not yet?

CYCLOPS
I see all.
Everything.
You believe I see all?

ODYSSEUS
No.

CYCLOPS
No?

ODYSSEUS
You don't see anybody.

CYCLOPS
I see you.

ODYSSEUS
I'm Nobody.

CYCLOPS (*Laughing*)
So you said.

ODYSSEUS
All you see is nobody and nothing.

CYCLOPS
The Eye likes you.

ODYSSEUS
The ugliest thing is a liar. So you're really ugly, sir.

CYCLOPS
Noooh?
How ugly am I?
(ODYSSEUS *dances*.)

ODYSSEUS
Man, you so ugly nobody would believe it.

CYCLOPS
Except you.

ODYSSEUS (*Black accent*)
I'm nobody, dude. You're *ugly*, I believe it.

CYCLOPS (*Roaring with laughter*)
God, what accent is that? I'm going to die.

ODYSSEUS
Oh, you will, you will, boss.

CYCLOPS (*Weeping with laughter*)
                                        Stop, you're making me cry.

ODYSSEUS
Laughter and tears, right? Pouring from the one eye.

CYCLOPS
I'm exhausted. You're funny. I'll see you again.

ODYSSEUS
Not if I see you first, man.

CYCLOPS
                              You're a killer, Nobody.

ODYSSEUS (*Laughing*)
Not as much as you, my man.

CYCLOPS
You're coming to dinner.

ODYSSEUS
I thought I *was* dinner.
(*The* CYCLOPS *exits, roaring with laughter.* EURYLOCHUS
and the two SAILORS *get up and join* ODYSSEUS.)

EURYLOCHUS
What do we do now? Think, Captain Odysseus!

FIRST SAILOR
You must have some ideas: you're famous for scheming.

ODYSSEUS
Let me think, let me think. There's some way out of this.

SECOND SAILOR
They're coming back. Oh God! Let us all be dreaming!
(*The* PATROLMEN *return.*)

FIRST SAILOR
Come on, then. They need us. Don't whimper, don't bend.

EURYLOCHUS
Generations of men, like seeds flung on the wind.
(ODYSSEUS *obstructs a* PATROLMAN.)

66

ODYSSEUS
Listen, the Cyclops likes me, sir, I'm his good friend.
FIRST SAILOR
Oh God, sir! Oh God, please, Captain.
ODYSSEUS

> Leave him behind!

(*The* SAILORS *and* EURYLOCHUS *are removed.*)

SCENE IX

A dinner table. Night. ODYSSEUS *and the* CYCLOPS *eating, attended by* RAM, *a manservant.*

CYCLOPS
Know what you're eating? Your men. As good as sheep.
(ODYSSEUS *pauses, eats.*)
ODYSSEUS
And you know what they call these drops from my eyes?
Tears.
(*He stops eating.*)
CYCLOPS
My eyes cloud when I laugh. You must teach me to weep.
ODYSSEUS
Well, first you must lose things you loved.
CYCLOPS

> Then cry, like this?

(*He squeezes his eye shut.*)
ODYSSEUS
Not quite.
CYCLOPS (*Opening his eye*)
I like laughing. Make me laugh, little man.
ODYSSEUS
Make you laugh. All right. Know why I can cross my eyes?
(*He crosses his eyes.*)

CYCLOPS (*Giggling*)
    No, why?
ODYSSEUS
                God gave us two eyes because we're human.
CYCLOPS
    I'm not.
ODYSSEUS
                One is for laughter, the other one cries.
CYCLOPS
    Do it. Show me. Ram, come here. Take a look at this.
    (ODYSSEUS *makes a funny face.* RAM *comes forward.*)
RAM
    Very good, sir. Nobody I know can do it.
    (*He resumes his position.*)
CYCLOPS
    I love Nobody.
ODYSSEUS
                Same here. Nobody loves you.
CYCLOPS
    Look! Why do you need two eyes? One does just as well.
ODYSSEUS
    For balance. Proportion. Contrast. Mortals need two.
CYCLOPS
    I'm a demi-god.
ODYSSEUS
                Left, right. Good, bad. Heaven, hell.
CYCLOPS
    I have deified myself. Son of Poseidon.
ODYSSEUS
    I know your father, the sea. He doesn't like me.
CYCLOPS
    Why? I'll talk to him.
ODYSSEUS
                Gods! Who knows what side they're on?
CYCLOPS
    He's rough-tempered most times, but he can act calmly.

ODYSSEUS
Put in a good word, then. I'm trying to get home.
CYCLOPS
Home. You're home now.
ODYSSEUS
                              Well, this wasn't quite my idea.
(*Silence.*)
CYCLOPS
Not your idea? There're no ideas in this kingdom.
ODYSSEUS
I've a wife, you see. Like my eyes. We make one pair.
CYCLOPS
Where's that, my little friend? Tell me where you come
    from.
ODYSSEUS
A rock, too stony for horses. With swirling shores . . .
CYCLOPS
What flocks do you have? Goats, sheep? Is it a kingdom?
ODYSSEUS
Yes.
CYCLOPS
    And are you its king?
ODYSSEUS
                              Yes. But it's not like yours.
CYCLOPS
In what way?
ODYSSEUS
            Its subjects don't end up on skewers.
CYCLOPS (*Laughs*)
Like your men, you mean?
ODYSSEUS
                        Right.
CYCLOPS
                        How many've I eaten?
ODYSSEUS
Of my crew? Just two. I suppose, before them, scores.

69

CYCLOPS
They're tenderized by tortures, the flesh is beaten.
ODYSSEUS
While your sheep bleat in fear of their devourer.
CYCLOPS
But I'm saving you for last.
ODYSSEUS
Well, that's very kind.
CYCLOPS
Thank you.
ODYSSEUS
Two of my crew, and one philosopher.
(*The* CYCLOPS *picks his teeth.*)
CYCLOPS (*Spits*)
Is this him?
No more ideas. The last of his kind.
(ODYSSEUS *holds the skewer over the flame.*)
ODYSSEUS
Look how this little iron lance glows at the tip!
CYCLOPS
Stick it in the meat.
(ODYSSEUS *drops the skewer.*)
ODYSSEUS
Too hot.
CYCLOPS
Ram, get a clean one.
(ODYSSEUS *searches on his knees for the skewer, hiding it.*)
ODYSSEUS
No, no, no, it's all right, really. I'll pick it up.
CYCLOPS
Ram, a clean skewer!
ODYSSEUS (*From under the table*)
No, really.
CYCLOPS
LEAVE IT ALONE!

(RAM *exits.* ODYSSEUS, *on his knees looking, gets near the door.*)
ODYSSEUS
That's the way I am, sorry. I hate losing things.
CYCLOPS
GET OFF YOUR KNEES!
ODYSSEUS
My men, my money. My way home.
CYCLOPS
Your life next.
ODYSSEUS
That I don't mind. Just hate losing things.
CYCLOPS (*Searching, on his knees*)
I'll help you look.
ODYSSEUS
That's three eyes, fine. Where did it go?
CYCLOPS
It couldn't have gone far. And Ram will be back soon.
ODYSSEUS
I give up. But I hate to. One thing you should know.
CYCLOPS
What's that?
ODYSSEUS
The sky goes pitch black when there is no moon.
(*He crawls near the* CYCLOPS, *takes out the skewer, blinds him.*

Blackout. Sirens moaning.)
CYCLOPS
NOBODY HAS ESCAPED, NOBODY BLINDED
    ME!
LOUDSPEAKER
REPEAT, NO ONE HAS ESCAPED. KEEP
    LOOKING FOR HIM.
NOBODY'S ESCAPED, NOBODY'S BLINDED THE
    EYE.

CYCLOPS
NOBODY, YOU HEAR ME? NOBODY IS HIS
NAME!
ODYSSEUS (*Shouts back*)
SON OF POSEIDON! YOU OBSCENE OCTOPUS!
YOU TON OF SQUID-SHIT, WITH YOUR EYE
POURING BLACK INK!
MY NAME IS NOT NOBODY! IT'S ODYSSEUS!
AND LEARN, YOU BLOODY TYRANTS, THAT
MEN CAN STILL THINK!
(*Sirens moan. The* CYCLOPS *picks up an oil drum and hurls
it at the retreating* ODYSSEUS, *screaming.*)

SCENE X

*Circe's island. A beach. Rich wild plantains. Some of the
crew lolling. A* WOMAN *playing a drum.* ODYSSEUS *and*
EURYLOCHUS *enter.*

FIRST SAILOR
Circle the graves of our bodies, traveller. Pass.
(ODYSSEUS *crouches near a* SAILOR .)
ODYSSEUS
Sailor, this sudden indifference, where's it from?
FIRST SAILOR
That red flower nodding agreement with the grass.
ODYSSEUS
A sleeping sickness. They were felled by its perfume.
EURYLOCHUS
You went ashore for fresh water! Back to the ship!
ODYSSEUS
The island has drugged them. They've no will to go on.
EURYLOCHUS
Their heads hang like sunflowers.
(*He shakes a* SAILOR.)

72

FIRST SAILOR

                            Tell the sea to sleep.

SECOND SAILOR

Here the lion takes a whole afternoon to yawn.

THIRD SAILOR

Join us, Captain. Watching you stand makes us tired.

EURYLOCHUS

What have you eaten? What changed you? What is this
    place?

THIRD SAILOR

This place? An island that has all you desired.

ODYSSEUS

It's the falls.

EURYLOCHUS

            What?

ODYSSEUS

                That waterfall, thundering peace.

EURYLOCHUS

Could its veils bind their limbs like this?

ODYSSEUS

                            And mine.

(EURYLOCHUS *shoves* ODYSSEUS.)

EURYLOCHUS

                                Move! Move!

ODYSSEUS

Although my longing for home is as strong as theirs.

EURYLOCHUS

Captain, keep moving.

(ODYSSEUS *slides down*.)

ODYSSEUS

                So great . . . this burden called love.

(EURYLOCHUS *lifts* ODYSSEUS.)

EURYLOCHUS

Up! Up!

FIRST SAILOR

    Yield like a lily to the weight of years.

73

SECOND SAILOR
All forms of love are meaningless except self-love.
EURYLOCHUS
Who did this?
THE WOMAN
Circe.
FIRST SAILOR
Don't breathe, Captain. What's the rush?
SECOND SAILOR
The grave is coming towards us. No need to move.
THIRD SAILOR
The grave we all come from was hidden by a bush.
FIRST SAILOR
Then Doubt went into labour and produced Reason.
EURYLOCHUS
What is in this weed that makes fools philosophers?
ODYSSEUS
My head's clearing now. Like a mist burnt by the sun.
EURYLOCHUS
All right, men. Back to the ship. It's waiting for us.
FIRST SAILOR
Flowers, like fire.
EURYLOCHUS
Try, sailor. How do you feel?
FIRST SAILOR
In a different archipelago. But the same.
SECOND SAILOR
They worship the elements. They kneel like you kneel.
THIRD SAILOR
Each god has his earthen root.
SECOND SAILOR
Just a different name.
FIRST SAILOR
Their gods quarrel like ours and hurl meteors.
SECOND SAILOR
They sacrifice oxen. Drink their blood from clay bowls.

FIRST SAILOR
They spin, possessed, around delirious altars.
THIRD SAILOR
Then wound the earth and descend to the place of souls.
(*Music.* REVELLERS *enter, with animal masks, singing.*)
CHORUS (*Sings*)
Aeaea
Aeaea
Aeaea
Ai-ya-yi
My emerald island
Between blue sea, and blue sky
The island of Calypso
Aeaea
Ai-ee-o
Bacchanal
And carnival
Is the place to go
O Lord have mercy
Before I dead
Let me lie down with Miss Circe
Stroking me head
Stroking me bald head
That have only one eye
When she stops
See me Cyclops
Falling down dead
O Lord have mercy
On all me sins, is true
But when Circe spell fell on me
I turn beast too.
(CIRCE *appears on a palanquin, carried by pig-headed*
BEARERS.)
Circe have mercy
Make me turn beast too.

Red decor. CIRCE *in her brothel, with* SAILORS *in the form of pig-men, and* GIRLS. BILLY BLUE, ODYSSEUS *and* EURYLOCHUS *enter.*

EURYLOCHUS
Madame, we'd like our crew back.
ODYSSEUS

                                   With your permission.
CIRCE
Ever seen this before?
ODYSSEUS

                         Not quite.
CIRCE

                              You like watching?
ODYSSEUS
Not my men.
CIRCE

                 You see men? Sorry. Semen. I see swine.
(*She laughs.*)
EURYLOCHUS
This powerful weed metamorphosizes men.
CIRCE
The inner animal erupts through their features.
ODYSSEUS
Her black locks pouring like a golden lion's mane.
EURYLOCHUS
Spines bristle their backs, they have little obscene eyes.
CIRCE
But what they become is for what their natures yearned.
(*She strolls among the creatures, poking them with her wand.* ODYSSEUS *and* EURYLOCHUS *walk through the crowd. Grunts, screeches, off.*)
EURYLOCHUS
Her music's pounding with the odours of rutting.

ODYSSEUS
Perfumes won't dispel it.
EURYLOCHUS
Her rooms are grunting pens.
ODYSSEUS
Still, give it to our enchantress, she knows one thing.
EURYLOCHUS
What?
ODYSSEUS
That brothels aren't just sailors' dreams, but all men's.
EURYLOCHUS
Not mine.
ODYSSEUS
All.
EURYLOCHUS
Don't yield, sir, you have a wife and son.
ODYSSEUS
At the back of all men's minds is a rented room.
EURYLOCHUS
Her hatred can be dispelled. She thinks men are swine.
ODYSSEUS
We create our own features. Not her. We change form.
(ATHENA *appears, offers a flower, blocks* ODYSSEUS.)
ATHENA
Wait. Chew this milky flower. They call it moly.
ODYSSEUS
What is its power?
ATHENA
Chew it, you're out of her range.
ODYSSEUS
Where did you find it? It's streaked. The sap looks milky.
ATHENA
In a speckled grove. Gods know it. Chew it, or change.
ODYSSEUS (*To* EURYLOCHUS)
Have you eaten it?

EURYLOCHUS
                    Not yet.
ODYSSEUS
                              Will it work?
EURYLOCHUS
                                        Yes, yes.
ODYSSEUS
Look, it may be great to be a pig for a change.
EURYLOCHUS
With grunts for a language, a screw prick, bristling ears?
ODYSSEUS (*Chews*)
Cheers.
EURYLOCHUS
            Here comes our hostess with her fatal hors d'oeuvres.
(CIRCE *approaches*.)
CIRCE
Have you had one of these yet? They're lovely with wine.
ODYSSEUS
No, they look lovely. Your own little endeavours?
CIRCE
My own little hands.
(*Claps her hands*.)
        NOW, BACK TO YOUR STIES, YOU SWINE!
(*She herds the pig-men off, then takes* ODYSSEUS' *hand*.)
ODYSSEUS
Where're we going, madame, and what about my friend?
CIRCE
Let him find his own diversions. Rent his own room.
ODYSSEUS (*To* EURYLOCHUS)
This is for the crew's sake.
CIRCE
                              We won't be hard to find.
EURYLOCHUS
But where?
CIRCE
            Where, except down a woman's path? Perfume.

(ODYSSEUS *and* CIRCE *exit, two* GIRLS *accost*
EURYLOCHUS.)

FIRST GIRL
What's up, Mr Gentleman? Look a little lost.

SECOND GIRL
How you feelin', sailor? What's this in your pocket?

EURYLOCHUS
I don't care to be accosted, thank you.

FIRST GIRL
                                    No cost.

(EURYLOCHUS *searches his clothes.*)

SECOND GIRL
What are you feeling for in your pocket?

EURYLOCHUS
                                    It's gone.

SECOND GIRL
You lost it?

EURYLOCHUS
            A flower.

SECOND GIRL
                    Let me pick it.

(*She fondles* EURYLOCHUS, *while the* FIRST GIRL *forces a
drink down his throat. They step back.* EURYLOCHUS
*changes into a pig. They laugh, chase, catch him, one rides
him, the other puts a garland around his neck and drags
him off squealing.*)

                    SCENE XII

Interior. CIRCE *prepares Odysseus' drink, slipping in a
powder. He chews the moly-flower.* BILLY BLUE *enters.*

BILLY BLUE (*Sings*)
She give him shining bush to drink, she give him man-you-
    must

79

She fix him a liqueur of gooseberry wine
But his flag still at half mast
She pour in some sweet-oil and crush it with thyme
Coriander, basil and cerasee
But the flower of the moly slowly defy she
Power of matrimony
No, no, doux-doux
I have a message for you
As sweet as you are
And you sweeter than guava jam
I have a wife at home
And she begging me come
And I saving it all for she.
(ODYSSEUS *sips the potion.* CIRCE *is undressing slowly.*)
I have a wife at home
And she begging me come
And I saving it all for she.
She slip off she shoulder strap, she raise up she hem
She untangle she jewellery
All the time she keeping her big black eyes on him
Circe circling him for some revelry
With lavender, rosewater and cerasee
But the moly slowly, slowly strengthening him
He thinking as he drinking
No, no, doux-doux
I have a message for you
As fresh as you are
And you sweeter than sugar-plum
I have a wife at home
And she begging me come
So I saving it all for she.
CIRCE
Become this man to whom everything has happened.
ODYSSEUS
What I want is so simple. To reach my own bed.

CIRCE
You'll learn more than the others. The swine I keep penned.
ODYSSEUS
What would I learn from this?
CIRCE
From a goddess? Godhead.
ODYSSEUS
But taking what form if not a man's any more?
CIRCE
My nostrils flared the minute I saw you enter.
ODYSSEUS
Why?
CIRCE
Your head lifted. A stallion circling his mare.
ODYSSEUS
With your season on the wind?
CIRCE
Circling. Thudding her.
ODYSSEUS
This stallion's married.
(CIRCE *strokes his thigh*.)
CIRCE
What did this?
ODYSSEUS
Boar. Hunting scar.
CIRCE
Hunt mine. We're kindred spirits.
ODYSSEUS
Yes?
CIRCE
You know we are.
ODYSSEUS
Not kindred bodies. This pig-scarred adventurer.
CIRCE
Reason has never restrained you, Odysseus.
(ATHENA *enters, disguised as a maid*.)

ODYSSEUS
We have company.

CIRCE
                    She's young. You'd like to try her?

ODYSSEUS
As well? Too exhausting.

CIRCE
                    Go about your business!

(ATHENA *exits*.)

ODYSSEUS
Madame, I'm sure this could be a night well spent.

CIRCE
You're in your house. A house men's desires built.

ODYSSEUS
Paradoxes in brothels. Why's this different?

CIRCE
Deceit without sadness.

ODYSSEUS
                    Only swine feel no guilt.

CIRCE
When heaven flares from the charge of our joined bodies.

ODYSSEUS
What?

CIRCE
          Your spasm's force need not bring oblivion.

ODYSSEUS
And my wife?

CIRCE
                    My cold lips will be Penelope's.

ODYSSEUS
Ah!

CIRCE
          We'll re-create the gendering of your son.

ODYSSEUS
No 'home' and no mercy. The white harbour. The heat.
(CIRCE *lifts the bedsheet*.)

CIRCE
After rough seas, rest. From this tangled linen, calm.
ODYSSEUS
To lie on my olive-tree bed, sun crossing its sheet.
CIRCE
Rest your head on the length of this ebony arm.
(*She licks his body and rolls over. They make love, then sleep.* ATHENA *enters as a servant. She draws a circle around their bed, sprinkling it with flour, hides.* CIRCE *leaps up.*)
ODYSSEUS
What's wrong? You just leapt out of bed like a whirlwind.
CIRCE
Someone was here.
(*She rises, paces, distracted.*)
ODYSSEUS
     The sheets are all soaked with your sweat.
CIRCE
I heard: 'You're a monstrous bitch. You'll pay in the end.'
ODYSSEUS
Who?
CIRCE
    A green-eyed goddess. You're her favourite.
ODYSSEUS
Who was she?
CIRCE
      She sprinkled it round this bed. White sand.
ODYSSEUS (*Tasting it*)
It's not sand, it's flour.
CIRCE
     That girl crept back in here.
ODYSSEUS
You heard her whisper something? I didn't hear a sound.
CIRCE
We're ringed by an owl's cold eye. Death is its centre.

ODYSSEUS
The forest is thick with branches where wild owls brood.

CIRCE
And they are her heralds. Maman de l'Eau. Athena.

ODYSSEUS
You're cold as a corpse.

CIRCE
                        A vision has iced my blood.

ODYSSEUS
Then change my men back.

CIRCE
                        A white owl with lids of stone.

ODYSSEUS
So, an owl flew in. Not all owls are an omen.
(ATHENA *exits.*)

CIRCE
She hides in a waterfall's cascading curtain.

ODYSSEUS
Maybe she wants you to turn your swine back to men.

CIRCE
Her words kept bubbling like a pool's cold basin.

ODYSSEUS
Muttering nonsense.

CIRCE
                        That you were her chosen man.

ODYSSEUS
What about my men?

CIRCE
                        Remorse will change them from swine.
(*She huddles in a corner, moaning.*)

ODYSSEUS
Don't huddle there like a little girl, please; don't moan.

CIRCE
A RIVER OF FIRE, A RIVER OF LAMENTATION!

ODYSSEUS
Wake up! You were dreaming.

CIRCE
                              You must go down to hell.
ODYSSEUS
  Child! Hell is the shadow of imagination.
  (*Points to the window-curtain billowing.*)
CIRCE
  Look! Look at that curtain.
ODYSSEUS
                              Now it lifts like a sail.
  (CIRCE *looks under a pillow for a pack of cards, spreads
  them, holds one up in fear.*)
CIRCE
  Let me trace your palm's rivers. Sit; open to me.
ODYSSEUS
  I don't believe in that hoodoo, or in this card.
  (*He shows his palm.* CIRCE *reads it.*)
CIRCE
  A cock to Shango or sombre Persephone.
ODYSSEUS
  Some plumed rooster like Ajax strutting in your yard?
  (CIRCE *kisses him.*)
CIRCE
  Love, in this world where my body was your compass.
ODYSSEUS
  Where I've spun for twenty years without my true north.
CIRCE
  Enter the magnetic earth through which our souls pass.
ODYSSEUS
  Why?
CIRCE
                              Eternity's lost. My mouth leeched to your mouth.
  (*She kisses him again.*)
ODYSSEUS
  Suppose it wasn't prophecy but a bad dream?
CIRCE
  No.

ODYSSEUS
  You're trembling. Come, I'll lift the cloud of your hair.
CIRCE
  I saw black Acheron fuming, that stinking stream.
ODYSSEUS
  But those who cross to its bank can go no farther.
CIRCE
  Their faces will turn to meet yours. Enemy, friend.
ODYSSEUS
  I shall greet the dead?
CIRCE
                    Dig this trench. Long as your arm.
ODYSSEUS
  You're mad!
CIRCE
                You'll see a blind man shawled in a black wind.
ODYSSEUS
  I thought only pigs saw the wind. In your pig farm.
CIRCE
  You'll sprinkle this raw trench with wild barley and milk.
ODYSSEUS
  Persephone's rites. You know what my nightmare was?
CIRCE
  What?
ODYSSEUS
      To drown in this oblivion of scented silk.
  (*He yanks off the sheets.*)
CIRCE
  Drown? Didn't the rustle of linen please your ears?
ODYSSEUS
  Carried far from my coast on pillows of lace-foam.
  (*He tears open the pillows.*)
CIRCE
  Go home, then!
ODYSSEUS (*Barking*)
  Yap, yap! Licking your feet like a dog.

CIRCE
    Finished?
ODYSSEUS
                Clicking your fingers. 'Come when I say "Come!"'
CIRCE
    But I loved you, my pet.
ODYSSEUS
                    Good. Unleash him. Your dog.

                    SCENE XIII

A yard. DRUMMERS, SHANGO DANCERS *in white, with
candles, a sacrificial rooster swung by the neck as a circle of
chalk is drawn on the ground by* PRIESTS, *and* ODYSSEUS,
*in an admiral's uniform under his great-coat, is given a
sceptre and a wooden sword, as* CIRCE *leads him to the
centre of the chalk circle.*

CELEBRANTS (*Chanting, dancing*)
    Shango
    Zeus
    Who see us
    Man go
    Name Odysseus
    Go down
    Go down
    Ogun
    Erzulie
    Go down to hell
    Sprinkle water
    Erzulie
    Athena
    Maman d'l'Eau
    River Daughter
    Shango

                    87

Zeus
All who see us.

CIRCE
Your soundless sword will divide not only the air.

SHANGO PRIEST
Severing this world of light from one past knowing.

CIRCE
Where buried Persephone glides for half the year.

SHANGO PRIEST
Till helmets of gold crocuses shoot with the spring.

CIRCE
As this blade divides the world from the underworld.

SECOND SHANGO PRIEST
So the hairline of one breath keeps body from soul.

CIRCE
O world halved by absence, by Time's exacting sword!

SECOND SHANGO PRIEST
While both worlds keep yearning to make each other whole.

CIRCE
Go, where the chosen of gods alone can enter.

SECOND SHANGO PRIEST
This crack in the heart-broken earth, here you descend.

CIRCE
Tell green-eyed Athena I'll never offend her.

ODYSSEUS
And my crew?

CIRCE
                    Restored. Our life ends in a black wind.
(ODYSSEUS' *eyes are wrapped in a black cloth.*)

FIRST SHANGO PRIEST
You dig a trench. This long. (*Showing an arm.*)

CIRCE
                         You must wound the ground.

ODYSSEUS
With what?

CIRCE

This sword. It'll open. A woman stands there.

ODYSSEUS

Who?

CIRCE

A phantom on a platform. An iron sound.
(*Sound of huge door opening.*)

FIRST SHANGO PRIEST

Earth's stomach.

CIRCE

A widowed phantom. Your dead mother.

ODYSSEUS (*In tears*)

You swine!
(*He swings the wooden sword.*)

CIRCE

To see her, enter this divided stone . . .

ODYSSEUS

Why this heart-breaking vision? Why not another?

CIRCE

A station, echoing arches. And her, alone.
(ODYSSEUS *draws an 'L' on the earth. The* CELEBRANTS
and CIRCE *withdraw. The earth opens.*)

SCENE XIV

The Underground. ODYSSEUS *removes his bandage, enters
the turnstile. A machine with a mirror. Then, behind him, a
woman in a coat, hat and scarf: his mother,* ANTICLEA.

ANTICLEA

Is it running late? These days they've been running late.

ODYSSEUS

Don't you recognize me?

ANTICLEA

Who are you?

89

ODYSSEUS

Mama, I'm your son.

ANTICLEA

Odysseus? You're now one of our bodiless freight?

ODYSSEUS

No. I'm not dead. Now I pray that I will be soon.

ANTICLEA

Well, one's no worse than the other.

ODYSSEUS

When I look in a mirror . . .

ANTICLEA

Yes?

ODYSSEUS

I see the skin wrinkling at my throat now; like yours.

ANTICLEA

If I looked in a mirror there'd be nothing there.

ODYSSEUS

Not the 'you' that I find in me over the years?

ANTICLEA

Is that how I smiled? Did I toss my chin like that?

ODYSSEUS

Every mirror echoes it. Your mannerisms.

ANTICLEA

Including this one? 'Boy, I'll give you a big clout.'
(*She pretends to strike him, smiling.*)

ODYSSEUS

My tears multiply you as if they were prisms.
(*He weeps.*)
Why're you here alone? Why're you waiting around?

ANTICLEA

It's my station. Under the bed of the river.

ODYSSEUS

How many more stations are there in the Underground?

ANTICLEA

You never get off. The train goes on forever.
(BILLY BLUE, *as a blind vagrant with his guitar,*

90

belongings and a stick, stops and puts out a palm.)
BILLY BLUE
Two coins for these white eyes, sir, and I'll prophesy.
ODYSSEUS
You live here?
BILLY BLUE
                    Correct. Sleep most nights under the bridge.
ODYSSEUS
Homeless?
BILLY BLUE
              No more than you, sir. So far as I see.
ODYSSEUS
How far's that?
BILLY BLUE
              The future.
ODYSSEUS
I doubt.
BILLY BLUE (*Shrugging*)
              Your priv'lege.
ODYSSEUS
I've no money. Time has broken me at great cost.
BILLY BLUE
Yeah, but the word 'home' swirls in the caves of your ears.
ODYSSEUS
Grief added to my fortune the mother I lost.
ANTICLEA
Just give him one coin. He hustles his prophecies.
(*A train flashes past.* ODYSSEUS *pays* BILLY BLUE.
TIRESIAS *enters.*)
ODYSSEUS
My comrades screamed in the window behind the glass.
TIRESIAS
Right. Heard what they were saying?
ODYSSEUS
                    No. Not a sound.

TIRESIAS
They were the open mouths of your crew. More will pass.
ODYSSEUS
When do they stop?
TIRESIAS
Their station. Wherever they sinned.
(ELPENOR *appears on the opposite platform, in a*
midshipman's uniform, with a bag, his head bandaged.)
ODYSSEUS
There, across these, what are these?
TIRESIAS
                                Tracks.
ODYSSEUS
                                           I'll talk to him.
ELPENOR
I couldn't bear to face you. I'm sorry, Captain.
ODYSSEUS
Dear boy, my other son! I still haven't reached home.
TIRESIAS
Wait, he's on the other platform, it's not your turn.
ELPENOR
I got drunk. I fell. The blades of the propeller.
ODYSSEUS
Elpenor, you precede me, but I'll come over.
ELPENOR
No! No, sir, not yet. Forgive that drunken error!
(*A train arrives.* ELPENOR *walks quickly towards it, not*
turning.)
ODYSSEUS
Then his body swirled away from us like an oar.
TIRESIAS
In that alphabet of souls, Ajax to Zeus.
ODYSSEUS
This 'O' will be nothing that is Odysseus.
ANTICLEA
No. Your house waits beyond the foam-shouldering seas.

TIRESIAS
Make it two coins. Two eyes for the fate of others.
(ODYSSEUS *pays a coin.* THERSITES *passes.*)
ODYSSEUS
Thersites?
TIRESIAS
Yes. His useless sword on one shoulder.
ODYSSEUS
Didn't he find peace?
TIRESIAS
Too much. His true home was war.
ODYSSEUS
All his exploits forgotten, this rusted soldier?
TIRESIAS
He'll reach for his wife from boredom and fall on her.
(AJAX *strides past, visored.* THERSITES *exits.*)
ODYSSEUS (*Shouts*)
AJAX!
TIRESIAS
He will not turn or unvisor his eyes.
ODYSSEUS
He will, for me.
TIRESIAS
His gaze scorches on what it falls.
ODYSSEUS
Great heart, are you still sullen that you lost that prize?
(AJAX *stops, turns, lifts his visor.*)
TIRESIAS
There.
ODYSSEUS
Achilles' shield! It's drowned!
(AJAX *turns, continues.*)
If that's how he feels.
(AJAX *exits.*)
TIRESIAS
Even in hell he cuts inferior shadows.

93

ODYSSEUS
He always strode as if earth were dung to his heels.
(AGAMEMNON *crosses, bleeding, in a net.*)
ODYSSEUS
This one?
TIRESIAS
Towered on his mound, mourning Achilles.
ODYSSEUS
Agamemnon?
TIRESIAS
His was the saddest of their fates.
ODYSSEUS
God, look how he writhes in a net! Gaffed. A clubbed shark.
ANTICLEA
His own wife did that to him. You see how he fights?
TIRESIAS
Visions can blind you. Better to grope through the dark.
(AGAMEMNON *exits.*)
ANTICLEA
Earth has its joys, though all those joys are above us.
(ACHILLES *runs past, helmeted, in light.*)
TIRESIAS
Achilles, lightly leaping through asphodel fields.
ANTICLEA
He's happy that his son survived war's victories.
TIRESIAS
Like a stag in spring, kicking flowers from its heels.
ODYSSEUS
Lucky father.
(ACHILLES *exits.*)
ANTICLEA
Don't blame Troy on one fickle wife.
TIRESIAS
She was its cause, not its root. You're under a field.
ANTICLEA
Where Time stalks circling with his remorseless scythe.

94

TIRESIAS
  Weeding graves for generations, his sack is filled.
ANTICLEA
  Being the determined gardener that he is.
TIRESIAS
  With brown pods of helmets, dried ferns of warriors.
ANTICLEA
  Flower-eyed Nausicaas and bristling Thersites.
TIRESIAS
  Raking in those leaves that autumn held in arrears.
ANTICLEA
  He felled me on earth, a tree with crippled branches.
ODYSSEUS
  Couldn't he have spared you a few extra leaves?
ANTICLEA
                                                Why?
TIRESIAS
  We don't understand this rage of life for answers.
ODYSSEUS
  Questions are in our nature.
ANTICLEA
                              Then end naturally.
TIRESIAS
  Look through that tangled rigging of roots above you.
ANTICLEA
  Through that crack of sunlight left by the sliding dirt.
TIRESIAS
  A figure, whose sorrow is to blindly love you.
ANTICLEA
  From dawn to the moon's white motion. Can you still doubt?
  (*Roots dangle, then a shaft of light.*)
TIRESIAS
  No. There through those roots that let in the light of earth.
ODYSSEUS
  A woman sobbing under olive trees, alone.

TIRESIAS
    Wait, till the leaves shift.
ODYSSEUS
                    I can't see clearly enough.
TIRESIAS
    Now?
ODYSSEUS
            Unh!
TIRESIAS
            Your wife.
ODYSSEUS
                    Each tear thuds my chest like a stone.
ANTICLEA
    Son . . .
ODYSSEUS
        How many seas before my sail slides its mast?
TIRESIAS
    More islands, more trials.
ODYSSEUS
                    And more years. I'm still hers?
ANTICLEA
    There isn't a rock on your own coast more steadfast.
ODYSSEUS
    Even though a long absence has earned her divorce?
ANTICLEA
    Like a bridal rock she veils and unveils herself.
TIRESIAS
    She's still besieged like Troy by those roaring suitors.
ANTICLEA
    She's a rare vase, out of a cat's reach, on its shelf.
TIRESIAS
    One day his leaping claws could snatch her. Antinous!
ANTICLEA
    She'd rather hurl herself and be smashed to pieces.
ODYSSEUS
    And the others? Telemachus? And my old nurse?

ANTICLEA
Plough the sea's furrows to reach them, Odysseus.
TIRESIAS
And you'll sit on your bench with leaves like the ocean,
ANTICLEA
Under the magnanimity of a broad oak,
TIRESIAS
Dispensing justice there, rewarding devotion,
ANTICLEA
Till the bright sea darkens your life's concluding arc.
(ANTICLEA *fading*.)
TIRESIAS
Grey age will creep through your body like the grey sea.
ODYSSEUS
I want to die, to hold you again, my mother!
ANTICLEA
Blessed is the storm-tossed heart that ends tranquilly.
TIRESIAS
One breath divides you from her who's already here.
ANTICLEA
Now I shall fade like an oak leaf in your garden,
TIRESIAS
A stone bench in the oaks, watching your hedges foam.
ANTICLEA
Merciless Poseidon will grant you his pardon.
ODYSSEUS
Elpenor saw all this, through a crack in the storm.
(*Trains flash past. Thunder. The sea.*)

ACT TWO

SCENE I

Noon. A raft. ODYSSEUS, *ragged, badly sunburnt, is
singing.*

ODYSSEUS
Let his story be told, he's a mariner bold,
The king of the tumbling foam. He's been scorched by the
    sun,
Bones cracked by the cold, but a long, long –
Sing his song, song a long, long way from . . .
(Stops, gathering strength for the word –)
                           Home.
(A row of fins passes the raft. Squeaking.)
Dolphins.
(Sings)
Let his story be told, he's a mariner bold . . .
(A fish leaps on to the raft. ODYSSEUS *scrambles, catches it.
Another fish. He wraps both carefully in his shirt for later.)*
Been scorched by the sun . . .
(Behind him, a MERMAID *with wet hair climbs aboard.*
ODYSSEUS *staggers, turns. Another* MERMAID, *identical,
appears. He speaks to them.)*
Sorry. Do me a favour. Back where you came from.
FIRST MERMAID *(Drying her hair)*
Why?
SECOND MERMAID
    Yes, why?
ODYSSEUS
        So I'll know heat hasn't cracked my skull.
FIRST MERMAID *(About her hair)*
It's knotted. Weeds.

99

SECOND MERMAID (*Helping her*)
>> Are you saying we aren't welcome?

ODYSSEUS
I've had too much raw fish, that's what.

FIRST MERMAID
>> We're beautiful.

ODYSSEUS
You're very beautiful. But you're talking fishes.

SECOND MERMAID
You caught us, love.

ODYSSEUS
>> I didn't.

FIRST MERMAID
>> No, we leapt on board.

SECOND MERMAID
Because we felt sorry for you, Odysseus.

FIRST MERMAID
Never dreamt of two girls together in one bed?

ODYSSEUS
Fishes? A technical problem, wouldn't you say?

FIRST MERMAID
There are ways.

SECOND MERMAID
>> And means. You know, like tipping the scales.

FIRST MERMAID
And stroking their glittering wet breasts? It's easy.

SECOND MERMAID
Fish mate with men. Look! We aren't just old fishwives' tales!

FIRST MERMAID
Mum was a dolphin. Dad hailed from Nicosia.

SECOND MERMAID
Notice the way his frown forks into an anchor?
(ODYSSEUS *grabs a fish from his shirt.*)

ODYSSEUS
You're both going back home.

BOTH MERMAIDS

                                We don't want to leave you!

ODYSSEUS

To fight madness with madness is the only cure.
(*He hurls one fish away. The* FIRST MERMAID *screeches,
dives overboard.*)

SECOND MERMAID

Go on. Tell people you saw us. Who'd believe you?
(ODYSSEUS *holds the second fish. The* SECOND MERMAID
*thrashes around on the raft, slippery. He throws her
overboard. Silence.* ODYSSEUS *looks into the water.*)

ODYSSEUS (*Sings*)

Let his stories be told, he's a mariner old,
And his head's turning white as the foam.
Scorched by the sun, cracked by the cold
And a long – sing the song –
And a long, long way from . . .
(*Weeps*)

                                Home.

(*The raft, becalmed. Thin fog. Drowned* SAILORS, *from his
crew, climb aboard.*)

STAVROS

You remember us, Captain? We sail with you once.

COSTA

We loosened the winds.

STAVROS

                        Stavros, sir, from the mountains.

STRATIS

We drift, homeless, down there.

TASSO

                                We rise with penitence.

COSTA

When the gale swept Elpenor . . . ?

ODYSSEUS

                                Fog has fouled my brains.

(*They work.*)

STRATIS
We come to help you steer past them rotten-tooth crags.

TASSO
Ever hear of the Sirens, Captain? Two old crones.

STRATIS
They crouch up there in a yellow field. Real bags.

TASSO
Know what they drag for kindling? Sailors' skeletons.

STAVROS
Like bone-bleached driftwood.

ODYSSEUS
You've drifted this far, Stavros?

TASSO
Their jaws hang like empty purses, but from them, songs . . .

STAVROS
You listen, Captain; you drown. Don't be curious.

COSTA
Rolled by changing currents, made homesick for our wrongs.

ODYSSEUS
Poor souls . . .

STRATIS
The shadow of your raft passed over us.

STAVROS
I hear man sing, I say: 'Captain Odysseus?'

COSTA
And I said to Stavros, 'Is that our captain's voice?'

STRATIS
'Why that man not reach home after so many years?'

TASSO (*Stamping on raft*)
This plank's gone rotten.

COSTA
Cap, this gaff isn't much good.

STAVROS
This pail make holes like a cheese. Shame on you, Captain.

COSTA (*Ear to the raft*)
There's a choir of sea-worms singing in this wood.

ODYSSEUS
Why're you doing this?
STRATIS
To fetch you home. Screw this tin.
(*Hurls away an old tin.*)
COSTA
Up them gull-hooked rocks, riddled with spray like sponges.
TASSO
They climb, one claw, then the next, above the surf's war.
COSTA
To settle for their song. Then, from their jaws' hinges,
STRATIS
Music comes, Captain, to break your heart with pleasure.
COSTA
See that herd of hills coming like foaming oxen?
TASSO
And those charging waves, the cattle of Poseidon?
COSTA
Look! They're scrambling up rocks to direct their song!
STRATIS
It pierces a hole in your ribbed heart, then you drown.
(*Music begins.*)
ODYSSEUS
Tie me to the mast! Cram wax into your ears. Quick!
STRATIS
I crying like snow melting into the rivers.
COSTA
Sir, you will forget your loved ones in that music.
STRATIS
Don't listen like we did, sir, don't be curious.
ODYSSEUS
Roll the beeswax till it gets hot and plug your ears!
(STRATIS *finds the wax.*)
COSTA
Don't do this, Captain. You've got to listen to us.
(*They tie* ODYSSEUS *to the mast.*)

103

ODYSSEUS
Tie me up, and if I scream, ignore my orders.

COSTA
He's hearing.

TASSO
He's screaming something.

STRATIS
YOU'RE DEAF. ROW HARD!

COSTA
STEER CLEAR OF THE SHALLOWS. IT'S PULLING
US LIKE ROPES.
(ODYSSEUS *soundlessly screaming.*)

STRATIS
HE CAN SHOUT TILL HIS LUNGS BLEED, BUT
YOU NEVER HEARD!

COSTA
WHAT?

STAVROS (*Weeping*)
A shepherd's flute, dividing blue mountain slopes.

ODYSSEUS
LET ME JOIN THEM, YOU BASTARDS. PLEASE,
PLEASE, CAN'T YOU HEAR?

STRATIS
KEEP ROWING, GOD DAMN YOU, WE'RE
PASSING THROUGH THEIR SONG.

COSTA
WON'T BE LONG NOW, CAPTAIN, VERY SOON
WE'LL BE CLEAR.

ODYSSEUS
TURN! SET ME DOWN OVER THERE, THAT'S
WHERE I BELONG.
(*They pass through.* ODYSSEUS, *still tied, has his head
down, sobbing.* STAVROS *revives.*)

STRATIS (*Removing the wax carefully*)
We're out of range now, Captain. Can you still hear it?

ODYSSEUS
    No.
STRATIS
    You've heard it and lived, and no man will again.
ODYSSEUS
    Oh, Stratis, I felt such joy, no soul could bear it!
STRATIS
    I know. Their song is smoke fluting from a mountain.
ODYSSEUS
    And, Costa, after this, any music is noise.
COSTA
    It fades from your ears. Like shells that lose the sea's voice.
ODYSSEUS
    Through the veils of their song, I saw my beloved's eyes.
COSTA
    Everything you loved or fought for was in that bliss.
ODYSSEUS
    How can I repay you phantoms for all your toils?
STRATIS
    This isn't finished. There's Scylla and Charybdis.
ODYSSEUS
    Where?
STRATIS (*Pointing*)
            Those dark cliffs dividing. Where the channel boils?
COSTA
    It's your only way home, Captain. You have no choice.
STRATIS
    These aren't just sailors' stories that swirl round shipwrecks.
COSTA
    Where those drifting rocks resound with their false thunder.
STRATIS
    Scylla, she gobbles dolphins, with six writhing necks.
COSTA
    And gargling Charybdis who sucks vessels under.

(*Night. Heavy crossing clouds, shadows on the sail. The*

crew keep watch. ODYSSEUS *curls up. On either side,*
Scylla and Charybdis. EURYCLEIA *is rocking a cradle, she*
and BILLY BLUE *sing in turn.*)
EURYCLEIA (*Sings*)
Sleep, my lickle pickney, don't 'fraid no monsters,
As me launch your lickle cradle into dreaming seas.

Close your eyes with songs me sing you, lickle Odysseus,
See how the tree of heaven shake down all its flowers.
(*A star pitches.*)
BILLY BLUE (*Sings*)
Sometimes, to swaying sea-stars, clouds slowly close,
Their motion making monsters who widen at will.
EURYCLEIA (*Sings*)
So, cradled in him comfort, a child see what grows
From his shadow to shapes on a nursery wall.
(ODYSSEUS *cowers, whining.*)
BILLY BLUE (*Sings*)
Doubt foams into dark forms feeding on phosphorus,
The waves sound like jaws chewing the night.

Sometimes friendly faces turn to fiendish horrors.
Scylla soared on one side, Charybdis on his right.
(*In the moonlight, the* CREW *turn into a six-headed*
monster that rises like a changing cloud.)
Now cackling like Kraken from her churning cauldron,
Her six heads searching for a sea-meal of men . . .

Giant jaws grinding like gates of yawning iron . . .
EURYCLEIA (*Sings*)
Are all of these monsters a child's imagination?
(*The six heads approach* ODYSSEUS.)
BILLY BLUE (*Sings*)
Or the madness of a mariner too long alone?
(ODYSSEUS *screams. They overturn the raft.*)

A SHEPHERD *on a rock watches as* SAILORS *carry* ODYSSEUS *ashore with his sacks.* NAUSICAA *in a cloak is waiting.* ODYSSEUS *sleeps throughout.*

NAUSICAA
His head rolls like a seaweed weary of motion.
FIRST SAILOR
Never seen a man sleep so deep. Here's all his things.
NAUSICAA
Burrow the shield like a turtle. Pile it with sand.
SECOND SAILOR
Good, miss.
(NAUSICAA *kisses* ODYSSEUS.)
NAUSICAA
    You're home at last. Last of Troy's tired kings.
(*She and* SAILORS *exit.*

Ithaca. Sunrise.)
ODYSSEUS
Shepherd, how did I get here? What island is this?
SHEPHERD
They cradled you in a shell to rest on this coast.
ODYSSEUS
There was this island, a girl, I told them stories.
SHEPHERD
Then slept for a week.
(*Pause.*)
ODYSSEUS
    My fortune! The shield! It's lost!
SHEPHERD
No, they buried it in the dry sand of that cave.
ODYSSEUS
Did divers paddle down to it? Am I sleeping?

SHEPHERD
  You're wide awake.
ODYSSEUS
                  They'll snatch it! The sea's claws!
SHEPHERD
                                    It's safe.
ODYSSEUS
  You're lying.
  (*The* SHEPHERD *shakes his head.*)
              My fortune's gone. That's why you're smiling.
SHEPHERD
  Go and look.
ODYSSEUS
              I'm afraid to. The sea's done them harm.
SHEPHERD
  Salt does its work. You expect them bright and shining?
ODYSSEUS
  Look, I've a kingdom to manage when I get home.
SHEPHERD
  Correct.
ODYSSEUS
              I'm not like the others. I'm a small king.
  (*He looks for his goods, finds them.*)
SHEPHERD
  Of this honeycombed rock which is your small kingdom.
ODYSSEUS
  Where?
SHEPHERD
              The sand under your cracked feet.
ODYSSEUS
                                  Ridiculous.
  (*He dusts and polishes his goods.*)
SHEPHERD
  You slept for a week, tight as a nut in its shell.
ODYSSEUS
  There was a girl. A generous king . . . Alcinous.

(*He holds up the shield.*)
Look at this!

SHEPHERD
        What?

ODYSSEUS (*Laughing*)
        The turtle shell's found its turtle.

SHEPHERD
Can you hear a crystal noise, clear and refreshing?

ODYSSEUS
I hear wind like surf swaying the sails of poplars.

SHEPHERD
This is Raven's Rock, next to Arethusa's spring.

ODYSSEUS
And those poplars are Mount Neriton's, I suppose?

SHEPHERD
What tongue are spring and poplar talking, can you tell?

ODYSSEUS
From the crackle of their consonants . . . Ithacan.

SHEPHERD
Why should they speak your tongue, green leaf and clear
    vowel?

ODYSSEUS
I am in Ithaca? I'm home?

SHEPHERD
        Weep, weary man.

(ODYSSEUS *weeps*.)

ODYSSEUS
Why for ten years did my head roar with the sea's noise?

SHEPHERD
Ask yourself, for ten years, what did the bitterns scream?

ODYSSEUS
All I know is, I'm sick of the sea's bitterness.

SHEPHERD
The waves were homeless, the bitterns envied your dream.

ODYSSEUS
My tears are the salt that drenches those shaken trees.

SHEPHERD
Turn. What is the hoarse shale of your own surf sighing?
SURF VOICES
Polumechanos, polutlas, polumetis, Odysseus.
Polumechanos, polutlas, polumetis, Odysseus.
SHEPHERD
That's you, man of evasions, man skilled at lying.
(*Birds sing.*)
ODYSSEUS
The swallows are screaming . . .
SHEPHERD
To deafen you with joy.
ODYSSEUS
I'm nobody.
SHEPHERD
Change into the nobody you were.
ODYSSEUS
You're not a shepherd, are you? You're Athena, boy.
SHEPHERD
Now grime your face with sand and act like a beggar.
ODYSSEUS
Why?
SHEPHERD
To save your house and your fortune. Hurry now.
(*Distant, then nearer, dogs yelping.*)
The old man's a good soul, but a bit talkative.
ODYSSEUS
Which old man?
SHEPHERD
Hear his dogs yapping? He herds your swine.
ODYSSEUS
Eumaeus. Poor Eumaeus! Is he still alive?
SHEPHERD
He won't be if you don't act to save wife and son.
(*He exits.* EUMAEUS *enters.*)

EUMAEUS
Ay! Back! Mash!
(*He throws stones. The dogs run off.*)
                    Lucky they didn't tear you to pieces.
ODYSSEUS
My friend . . .
EUMAEUS
                    Rip you to bone like teeth tearing a chop.
ODYSSEUS
Not much here but bone, sir. Very little to seize.
(*He collects his things, covers his head.*)
EUMAEUS
Odysseus, my master. For him they used to stop.
ODYSSEUS
Think it'll rain?
EUMAEUS
                    That's how rain starts. With a drizzle.
ODYSSEUS
What work do you do, sir?
EUMAEUS
                    Keep hogs. Name's Eumaeus.
(*The sky darkens. Rain.*)
ODYSSEUS
Those clouds are building a storm. God help every sail.
EUMAEUS
Know the sea well?
ODYSSEUS
                    Know it? Suffered it. For ten years.
EUMAEUS
You look like a turtle, poking out from that shell.
ODYSSEUS
A bitter friend said the same thing. Ten years ago.
EUMAEUS
Where's home?
ODYSSEUS
                    Home? Crete, Crete.

EUMAEUS

What's in the sack?

ODYSSEUS

Can't you tell?

EUMAEUS

Sounds like a tinker's fortune.

ODYSSEUS (*Laughs*)

Right. Crowns. Junk. You know.

(*They stop.*)

EUMAEUS

Look at those puddles lying like shields in the sun.

ODYSSEUS

Reflecting clouds and phantoms. Our passing travail.

EUMAEUS

Aye. Our shadows slide over them, and then we're gone.

ODYSSEUS

The earth is still swaying.

(*They move.*)

EUMAEUS

Well, here we are. My hovel.

(*He opens his hut door.*)

ODYSSEUS

So where can I put my goods so they can be safe?

EUMAEUS

Look, I can't guard them. I've too much to account for.

ODYSSEUS

How about back here? Away from the clawing surf?

EUMAEUS

Love rough, wet nights. Memories in rain and fire.

(*Distant noise of* SUITORS *quarrelling.*)

ODYSSEUS

What's that?

EUMAEUS

Not dogs, men. Eating roasts from white-tusked boars.

ODYSSEUS

Who're they?

EUMAEUS
       Suitors.
ODYSSEUS
            I'll settle for bread and cheese.
EUMAEUS
Not them. Sucklings revolving on cracking embers.
ODYSSEUS
I'm not jealous, I'm hungry.
EUMAEUS
           How far're you from?
ODYSSEUS
                    White seas.
EUMAEUS
Three hundred and sixty pigs left. Won't last the month.
ODYSSEUS
How long has that feast been raging?
EUMAEUS
              Over three years.
ODYSSEUS
Must cost you a fortune to stuff everyone's mouth.
EUMAEUS
Fortune is putting it thinly! My house is yours.
ODYSSEUS
Don't put yourself out.
EUMAEUS
        I've been put out already.
ODYSSEUS
Bread, cheese and this fire is fine. I'm no suitor.
EUMAEUS
She'd treat you well, even if you weren't, my lady.
ODYSSEUS
Maybe if I were a bit younger, I'd suit her?
EUMAEUS (*Laughs*)
No. She's got a husband. If he didn't die.

ODYSSEUS
How would he treat those bores, then, your Odysseus?
EUMAEUS
Skewer their hearts on one lance and roast their livers.
ODYSSEUS
That's a lot of hearts.
EUMAEUS
       Oh, we'd cut them down to size.
ODYSSEUS
We?
EUMAEUS
  We chased real boars, racing by white rivers.
(*He serves, watching* ODYSSEUS *eat.*)
ODYSSEUS
This is good. A long time since I've tasted such ham.
EUMAEUS
My pigs grow like wine-casks from acorns and fresh springs.
ODYSSEUS
But they eat your pigs when pigs should be eating them.
EUMAEUS (*Laughs*)
You remind me of him. He used to say such things.
(*He pours wine.*)
ODYSSEUS
Back to a broken kingdom. To brood on Troy's fire . . .
EUMAEUS
Were you in that war?
ODYSSEUS
       . . . and see Helen's hair. I was.
EUMAEUS
For a faithless wife. Isn't that what it was for?
ODYSSEUS
Among other things. The smoke has clouded its cause.
(*Silence.*)
EUMAEUS
I'd a wife, once.

ODYSSEUS
                        Still, the place prospers, Eumaeus.
EUMAEUS
    Aye. Odd, in her absence, larks rise. Grass keeps growing.
ODYSSEUS
    I've seen it myself. Nature's contempt for our loss.
EUMAEUS
    Sows, smiling on their sides, like barrels thick with grain.
ODYSSEUS
    While his own wife pines.
EUMAEUS
                        And their boy, Telemachus.
ODYSSEUS
    But he's at the palace protecting his mother?
EUMAEUS
    No. He fled from that pig-pen. Its screeching chaos.
ODYSSEUS
    But, God, knowing all that, how could he leave her there?
EUMAEUS
    Because they meant to kill him when he came of age.
ODYSSEUS
    The suitors?
EUMAEUS
                        And now his mother must make a choice.
ODYSSEUS
    Swine! Who'll kill them?
EUMAEUS
                        Not you. What's a beggar's rage?
ODYSSEUS
    But the boy is safe?
EUMAEUS
                    In Menelaus' palace.
ODYSSEUS
    Think it's hopeless?
EUMAEUS
                        Hopeless.

ODYSSEUS

                         Won't the son inherit?

EUMAEUS

No. Sea-hawks are circling to seize Telemachus.

ODYSSEUS

Listen to that wind outside, Eumaeus. You hear it?

EUMAEUS

And the fire's raging.

ODYSSEUS

                         Like Troy's. What a far cause!

EUMAEUS

A black-maned storm galloping with Troy's wild horses.

ODYSSEUS

Wilder since the war.

EUMAEUS

                         God, what a man! No men left.

ODYSSEUS

You loved him?

EUMAEUS

                         A natural man, Odysseus.

ODYSSEUS

I know he loves you.

EUMAEUS

                         It's passed. The moon's going to lift.

ODYSSEUS

Cities crumble like clouds. Troy's towers are no more.

EUMAEUS

Aye. The lances of wild grass march across its plain.

ODYSSEUS

The beetle climbs over its stones in its armour.

EUMAEUS

Aye.

ODYSSEUS

     And crickets sing in helmets before the rain.
     (*Thunder passing.*)

EUMAEUS

The storm's shipping oars. I loved long oars and fighting.

ODYSSEUS

You move quite nimbly for your age, though, wouldn't you say?

EUMAEUS

With the shanks of an egret, but its beak? Lightning.

ODYSSEUS

Mine thin like reeds now.

EUMAEUS

Well, we were great in our day.

(*They laugh.*)

ODYSSEUS

When next do you drive a herd up to the palace?

EUMAEUS

You mean when do I bring hogs to swine? Tomorrow.

ODYSSEUS

Take me with you.

EUMAEUS

No. It would lance your heart, that place.

ODYSSEUS

Who'd notice one more beggar in all that uproar?

EUMAEUS

True.

ODYSSEUS

You believe in the gods? In bright Athena?

EUMAEUS

Well, at my age you've very little left but faith.

ODYSSEUS

In all my trials I've sensed but never seen her.

EUMAEUS

She pours mist into valleys. She makes the sea froth.

ODYSSEUS

I've lost all sense of city. Isn't that sad?

EUMAEUS

A tight hill town. You'll see when we bring the order.

ODYSSEUS
I passed through it once.
EUMAEUS
                     Walls splashed by the olive's shade.
ODYSSEUS
Let's hope its sunlit road remembers my shadow.
(*He wraps the cloak around himself, exits, followed by*
EUMAEUS.)

SCENE III

ODYSSEUS *curled up under a rock, asleep. Loud wind, sea,*
then a shaft of light, and ATHENA, *radiant. The storm*
passes.

ODYSSEUS
He's shot his thunderbolts. Old Zeus. Your father.
ATHENA
The cold sand is puddled. Look into your heart's pool.
ODYSSEUS
I'd better not. I'd just cloud it with my anger.
ATHENA
Anger? At whom?
ODYSSEUS
                Your thundering daddy.
ATHENA
                             YOU FOOL!
ODYSSEUS
See?
ATHENA
He sees! His forked lightning fingers each offence.
ODYSSEUS
Each offence? I've tried surviving, that's all I've done.
(*Pause. He paces.*)
You have been my goddess and daughter, both at once.

118

ATHENA
And you're to him what Telemachus is, a son!

ODYSSEUS
I'm the cause of my own wretchedness?

ATHENA
Since Troy, since . . .

ODYSSEUS
No! You gods who keep quarrelling like spoilt children.

ATHENA
LOOK, MORTAL! I SIDED WITH YOU, DESPITE
YOUR SINS!

ODYSSEUS
What sins, dazzling Athena, marked me from men?

ATHENA
You mocked the immortal ones.

ODYSSEUS
Is that all you mean?

ATHENA
You are the first to question the constant shining!

ODYSSEUS
With good reason.

ATHENA
The first to discount each omen!

ODYSSEUS
On calm nights at sea I have seen the gods falling.

ATHENA
Mortal, if I were you, I'd start my confession.
(*Silence.*)

ODYSSEUS
My maddened crew butchered the oxen of the sun.

ATHENA
Why were your Greeks turned to statues, your ship a stone?

ODYSSEUS
All right! I gouged the Cyclops, son of Poseidon!

ATHENA
Why did your crew devour the sun god's oxen?

ODYSSEUS

Corn and red wine. We had them. And then they ran out.

ATHENA

Those lyre-horned cattle were dear to Hyperion.

ODYSSEUS

Why should men starve when gods have all they can eat?

ATHENA (*Laughs*)

Still, you've done well. You've obeyed all my instructions.

ODYSSEUS

I gave orders, so I can take them, wise Athena.

ATHENA

Good. If your tongue slips, you bring on their destructions.

ODYSSEUS

That will be hard.

ATHENA

Now change. Act! No one has seen you.

(ATHENA *fades.* ODYSSEUS *sits up from the dream. He paces the sand in the gale.* EUMAEUS *leads him.* BILLY BLUE *enters.*)

BILLY BLUE (*Sings*)

Imagine the bitter ecstasy of Odysseus.
Imagine, after a hard night, coming home to your door.

Multiply that night by one week, by a month, Lord Jesus,
Multiply that month by a year, and then a score.

So you and the sunrise are climbing up your front step,
And some tree you knew looks suddenly twenty years older.

But that's not what's happening, that's why the homecomer
    wept,
As he felt the fingers of dawn touching his shoulder.

Ain't your house no more, your dog, your old lady, your cat,
Your son, your chair, your old coffee-cup, you're a bum.

A doormat marked 'Welcome', they scrape their soles on
    your heart,

And you can't do nothing about it, wouldn't that be sump'n?
(EUMAEUS *leaves* ODYSSEUS.)
Twenty years, and you wind up a tramp, outside your own
  door.
Now, if you were that cat, tell me, brother, wouldn't you be
  sore?

Wouldn't you be sore? Come on now, brother. I would.
Man, I'd have their thighs for drumsticks, and for wine?
  Their blood!

SCENE IV

The palace kitchen. ODYSSEUS *and* BILLY BLUE *as*
DEMODOCUS *in different corners. Sound of the* SUITORS.

ODYSSEUS
Do these lords ever give charity to the poor?
DEMODOCUS
They're as tight-fisted as the roots of the olive.
ODYSSEUS
I'd like a simple answer, with no metaphor.
DEMODOCUS
Tight as crab's arses, then. Metaphor's how I live.
ODYSSEUS
Singing round the islands?
DEMODOCUS
                          Your tone is just like Troy's.
ODYSSEUS
I have never seen Troy.
DEMODOCUS
                  Nor I, Mr No-man.
ODYSSEUS
I wasn't at Troy.

DEMODOCUS
                    I never forget a voice.
ODYSSEUS
    No?
DEMODOCUS
    This wanderer spoke it, but hated poetry.
    (*Silence. He hisses.*)
    His name sounded like hissing surf. Odysseus.
ODYSSEUS
    Never heard of him. I've heard the surf swirling, though.
DEMODOCUS
    I can tell height from voices. You're about his size.
ODYSSEUS
    Really? You see Odysseus?
DEMODOCUS
                    Not see. I see through.
ODYSSEUS
    That's a strange dialect. What island are you from?
DEMODOCUS
    A far archipelago. Blue seas. Just like yours.
ODYSSEUS
    So you pick up various stories and you stitch them?
DEMODOCUS
    The sea speaks the same language around the world's shores.
ODYSSEUS
    I've been blinded, too. By the sea's blazing silver.
DEMODOCUS
    It's not quite the same, friend.
ODYSSEUS
                    I've put out a giant's eye.
DEMODOCUS
    So I heard.
ODYSSEUS
            Yes.
DEMODOCUS
            Man, you must be one mean mother.

ODYSSEUS
So's any man in desperate straits.
DEMODOCUS
                                    I fancy.
ODYSSEUS
Does she ever visit her kitchen?
DEMODOCUS
                                    Rarely, friend.
ODYSSEUS
For one glimpse of her my heart might lose all reason.
DEMODOCUS
But why her, man? Is her patience now a legend?
ODYSSEUS
Because I once held such a woman. And our son.
DEMODOCUS (*Sings*)
There is only one thing that I can compare her to:
She is like a green pine that never sways on its hill,

Whose leaves repeat the swaying of burly water
Rooted in its cleft, not sea-grape or forked myrtle

Is as steadfast. Twenty years after Troy's slaughter,
As a green pine will make a castle of herself

This pine will feed no man's fire with crackling boughs
Or nestle his vows, as other branches, swallows,

But on her height, in a meadow of cold flowers,
She has weathered a siege even longer than Troy's.
(PENELOPE *enters*.)
PENELOPE
Ignore this Egyptian. Blind, like all flatterers.
ODYSSEUS
It's the truth.
PENELOPE
                    Maybe. But when did truth make men wise?
ODYSSEUS
May I talk with you?

PENELOPE

Our house is kind to beggars.

(*She exits.*)

DEMODOCUS

She's a fine, bright soul. Her presence brightens my eyes.

ODYSSEUS

No woman's company could lighten me like hers.

DEMODOCUS

What's she look like?

ODYSSEUS

Wind, brightening an olive tree.

DEMODOCUS

What's that, if it isn't one of those metaphors?

ODYSSEUS

Right. I met her first, right?

DEMODOCUS

'Met her first.' That's funny.

(*Sings*)

But on her height, in a meadow of cold flowers,
She has weathered a siege even longer than Troy's.

(MELANTHO, *the housemaid, Nausicaa's double, passes,
trips on* ODYSSEUS, *kicks him.*)

MELANTHO

You nearly made me fall, you homeless parasite!

ODYSSEUS

Sorry. But, girl, have some respect for your elders.

MELANTHO

You wanted me to fall so you could see these thighs?

(*She sits astride* ODYSSEUS.)

Nice?

ODYSSEUS

You could be hanged for this obscene insolence.

(MELANTHO *rises.*)

MELANTHO

You're going to be whipped! Who'll hang me?

124

ODYSSEUS

Odysseus.

MELANTHO

Bleeeeh! (*She wiggles her tongue at him.*)

ODYSSEUS

Nausicaa's mirror. Corrupted innocence.

(EURYCLEIA *enters.*)

EURYCLEIA

Melantho, get back inside and clear the table.

MELANTHO

No, you crooked black bitch! I'm engaged to a prince.

EURYCLEIA

Go on! That hot red mouth go bring you in trouble.

MELANTHO

And you'll be six foot under before that happens.
(*She exits.*)

ODYSSEUS

This neglected marsh, this swamp and chaos of a house!

EURYCLEIA

Is years, sir, all this damned wilderness been going on!

ODYSSEUS

Where's their master?

EURYCLEIA

Master? You mean Telemachus?

DEMODOCUS

The boy can't control them. It's a hundred to one.
(*Two* SCULLERY MAIDS *pass with a small barrel of fish,
barefoot, their shifts wet.*)

FIRST MAID

I'm so sick of gutting fish! My arms are all scales.
(ODYSSEUS *rises.*)

ODYSSEUS

You're sisters. The same white arms. I've seen you before.

FIRST MAID

Frightful, isn't it? The way the old fool scowls?

125

SECOND MAID
Terrible, the way his frown forks like an anchor.
ODYSSEUS
One wiry noon, out there, on the purple water.
FIRST MAID
Get away, you bug-eyed lobster! Draw in your claws.
ODYSSEUS
Yes.
(*The* MAIDS *laugh.*)
       I was fishing and caught you. Where was it? Please?
EURYCLEIA
Set of scandalous prick-teasers.
(MAIDS *exit, laughing, throwing fishes.* ARNAEUS *enters, a huge swineherd with an eye-patch, in a filthy sheepskin.*)
                        What you want now?
ARNAEUS
Not you, you dried-up old stick. I just brought some in.
EURYCLEIA
Eumaeus' pigs are better.
ARNAEUS
                 Who says so, you sow?
EURYCLEIA
I say so.
ARNAEUS
      A dog's dying near the garbage bin.
(EURYCLEIA *exits.*)
ODYSSEUS
Hello.
(ARNAEUS *crosses to* ODYSSEUS.)
ARNAEUS
      'Hello, sir,' said the dog. And who are you?
ODYSSEUS
I'm nobody.
ARNAEUS
        We don't like nobodies round here.

ODYSSEUS
That could be.

ARNAEUS
                    What?

ODYSSEUS
                              I said that could be.

ARNAEUS
                                        Don't argue.

(ODYSSEUS *gives the Cyclops salute.*)

ODYSSEUS
Sir!

ARNAEUS
Don't be smart either. Don't come on sarcastic.

ODYSSEUS
What happened to your eye?

ARNAEUS
                              None of your goddamned business.

ODYSSEUS
You keep rams?

ARNAEUS
                    So?

ODYSSEUS
                              Didn't I put it out with a stake?

ARNAEUS
Oh, you did? I see. He's crazy. That wasn't nice.
(*Throws* ODYSSEUS *off his stool.*)

ODYSSEUS
You herded rams on the cliffs of the Cyclades.

ARNAEUS
Rams? You open your mouth and I'll ram it with swill!

ODYSSEUS
Don't you remember?

ARNAEUS
                    What?

ODYSSEUS
                              Us, pulling our oar-blades?

(ARNAEUS *empties slop over* ODYSSEUS.)

ARNAEUS
Enjoy.

ODYSSEUS
Throwing a ship-sized boulder from your hill?

ARNAEUS
What hill?!
(ODYSSEUS *leaps on* ARNAEUS *and they wrestle, all over the kitchen.* EURYCLEIA *enters.*)

EURYCLEIA
Damn commotion! Where you think this place is?

ARNAEUS
I'll crunch your eyeballs like these two eggs, do you hear?
(*Squeezes two eggs in his palms.*)

EURYCLEIA
Arnaeus, look your money. Go 'bout your business.
(ARNAEUS *takes his money, shoves* ODYSSEUS *away.*
ODYSSEUS *sits on the floor.*)

ARNAEUS
Rams! Cyclades!
(ARNAEUS *exits.* EUMAEUS *enters.*)

EUMAEUS
The old dog's dying by the garbage.

DEMODOCUS
It smells like garbage.

EUMAEUS
Fur moulting from its ribs.

ODYSSEUS
Argus?

EURYCLEIA
Him won't eat.
(*She exits.*)

EUMAEUS
It's the heartbreak of old age.

ODYSSEUS
Since when?

DEMODOCUS
     Since his master set out on the long ships.
(ODYSSEUS *walks outside. Silence.* EUMAEUS *touches*
BILLY BLUE's *shoulder.*)

EUMAEUS
The old dog's tottering to him on newborn legs.

BILLY BLUE
Argus?

EUMAEUS
     Nosing his thighs. He's cradling it. It's dead.

BILLY BLUE
It waited for this. Its master. This king who begs.

EUMAEUS
I loved him as much. A dog saw more than I did.

BILLY BLUE
This man dare not weep. Though roads and nights can be
  wet.

EUMAEUS
I fed him his own meat. Housed him in my own hut.

BILLY BLUE
I smelled the sea on him. You must keep his secret.

EUMAEUS
God, what a knot of pain he must have for a heart!
(EUMAEUS *and* BILLY BLUE *exit.* TELEMACHUS *enters,*
cowled, sits in silence. ODYSSEUS *enters.*)

ODYSSEUS
And where're you from, young man?
(*Silence.*)

TELEMACHUS
I'm from where everybody comes from. From my home.

ODYSSEUS
And where's that? I said, 'Where is that?'

TELEMACHUS
             Look, man, it's late.

ODYSSEUS
It's never too late, youngster.

(*Silence.*)

TELEMACHUS

So, where are you from?

ODYSSEUS

From home, as well.

TELEMACHUS

Then we're both from the same place. Great.

(*He exits.*)

SCENE V

A palace chamber. Dusk on the painted walls. PENELOPE
enters, sits at her loom, then ODYSSEUS *approaches.*

PENELOPE

Now the Pleiades sit to hear sailors' stories.

ODYSSEUS

Now the lucky wanderer staggers to his bed.

PENELOPE

My own bed is besieged by a hundred suitors.

ODYSSEUS

And I've left the sea. Its lace was my faithless bride.

PENELOPE

So, you knew my husband?

ODYSSEUS

I know Odysseus.

PENELOPE

You say 'know,' not 'knew'. Does that mean he isn't dead?

ODYSSEUS

He's turned into a name, wandering the white seas.

PENELOPE

I cannot wait for a name or warm it in bed.

ODYSSEUS

You gave him a brooch once. A hound pinning a fawn?

PENELOPE
  You saw that brooch?
ODYSSEUS
                        Yes.

PENELOPE
                        Did it keep him through the war?
ODYSSEUS
  Before every battle, he would kiss it often.
PENELOPE
  And you saw this?
ODYSSEUS
                        I swear it.
PENELOPE
                        Men have sworn before.
  (*Silence.*)
  May I work while we talk? It's soothing, the rhythm.
  (*She weaves. A roar from the* SUITORS.)
ODYSSEUS
  My house has dark rooms that I dare not examine.
PENELOPE
  Where's your house?
ODYSSEUS
                        Here. (*He touches his temple.*)
                        The crab moves with its property.
PENELOPE
  And turtles.
  (*A roar from the* SUITORS.)
ODYSSEUS
  The sea breeds monsters. None strange as men.
PENELOPE
  Where's the thread in those thoughts?
ODYSSEUS
                        In my mind's tapestry.
  (*Silence.* PENELOPE *working.*)
  The pattern is intricate. What's it you're making?

PENELOPE
    A shroud for Laertes.
ODYSSEUS
                        That your suitors wait for?
PENELOPE
    Yes. They cottoned on.
ODYSSEUS
                        To the time it was taking?
PENELOPE
    I'd unstitch it like a swallow's beak picking straw.
ODYSSEUS
    Swallows are my friends.
PENELOPE
                        There's a nest in this house.
ODYSSEUS
    I'll have a word with one. But they've seen for themselves.
PENELOPE
    You mean my devotion to the god Odysseus?
ODYSSEUS
    You think he's a god?
PENELOPE
                        To the girl I was. Nothing else.
ODYSSEUS
    But now?
PENELOPE
                No change. No change. Today I have to choose.
ODYSSEUS
    One of those people in there?
PENELOPE
                        Yes. My son's now mature.
ODYSSEUS
    Which one do you like best? That fellow Antinous?
PENELOPE
    I said once the shroud was finished I would be sure.
ODYSSEUS
    If I were younger I might have been one of those.

PENELOPE
  When I unveil myself I'll also shroud this face.
ODYSSEUS
  Why?
PENELOPE
      I said I'd choose one from a hundred husbands.
ODYSSEUS
  Once the shroud was finished? Marriage was its promise?
PENELOPE
  The death of one vow in another's wedding banns.
ODYSSEUS
  Still, you'll rule the kingdom next to your husband's side.
PENELOPE
  Then my son could be killed or disinherited.
ODYSSEUS
  So soon you will wear both veils, both widow and bride.
PENELOPE
  And lilacs will make a grave of my marriage bed.
  (*Silence.*)
  Are you crying? You're cold. Shall I light a fire?
ODYSSEUS
  No, let me sit here and drain this joy to the dregs.
PENELOPE
  What joy?
ODYSSEUS
          A gratitude that comforts desire.
PENELOPE
  And you were a king somewhere?
ODYSSEUS
                      Once. Now one who begs.
PENELOPE
  As blue sea shows at the end of a corridor?
ODYSSEUS
  Yes?
PENELOPE
      Then it turns leaden and the sky threatens rain?

133

ODYSSEUS
Meaning?

PENELOPE
That is my house since he left for his war.

ODYSSEUS
But that sea might brighten and your husband return.

PENELOPE
They say there're two gates through which our dreams are
portrayed.

ODYSSEUS
Yes. One is made of ivory, the other, horn.

PENELOPE
That the ivory's hopes are false and we are betrayed.

ODYSSEUS
And the horn delivers whatever it has shown.

PENELOPE
I dreamt again last night of him. Odysseus.

ODYSSEUS
Which gate swung open? The horn or the ivory?

PENELOPE
The horn. I dreamt that an eagle killed all my geese.

ODYSSEUS
Are you asking me to interpret?

PENELOPE
Yes. Help me.

ODYSSEUS
The squawking geese? Suitors.

PENELOPE
The eagle?

ODYSSEUS
Odysseus.

PENELOPE
Ah!

ODYSSEUS
He'd pile the dead like linen for your servants.

134

PENELOPE
My maids will dress you in clothes that were my husband's.
ODYSSEUS
I'm not fit, ma'am.
(PENELOPE *goes to the door, claps her hands.*)
PENELOPE
EURYCLEIA! You're in good hands.
ODYSSEUS
Yes.
PENELOPE
No faith is surer than this old Egyptian's.
ODYSSEUS
So, trust her faith.
PENELOPE
Not every owl is an omen.
(*She returns to the loom.*)
ODYSSEUS
Do you always miss him?
PENELOPE
Does the doe miss her young?
ODYSSEUS
Or an aged lion its mate? I know what you mean.
PENELOPE
I weave and unweave this thing with a little song.
ODYSSEUS
It might break my heart.
PENELOPE
Oh, it's short. It won't break long.
(*Sings*)
Just as the sea's shuttle weaves and unweaves her foam,
He lies lost in a battle with salt weeds around him.
But she weaves and she prays that he'll one day come home
As fine as she found him when their vows were one.
(*Speaks*)
Well, it's finished now. He's dead. Like my widowhood.

ODYSSEUS
And if he's not dead?

PENELOPE
                    Too late. I gave them my promise.

ODYSSEUS
Can't you wait?

PENELOPE
                    I cannot, I must honour my word.

ODYSSEUS
I curse the cause of your sorrow, Odysseus.
(EURYCLEIA *enters with a basin, cloths, oils.*)

EURYCLEIA
Lord, missis, me must wash this man foot?

PENELOPE
                              He's our guest.

EURYCLEIA
Your guest. Na mine.

PENELOPE
                    Treat him as if this were his house.

EURYCLEIA
Damn stinking-toe beggar.

PENELOPE
                    Then he'll be combed and dressed.
(*She exits.*)

EURYCLEIA
Maybe you go be the first one she bring to she bed.

ODYSSEUS
Watch your tongue!

EURYCLEIA
                    Wash your foot.
(*She rolls up* ODYSSEUS' *robe to the thighs.*)
                              Wait. How you get this scar?

ODYSSEUS
A trapped boar rattled through dry reeds and lanced this thigh.

EURYCLEIA
A boar? In the same place?

136

(*Falls back.*)
                              Oh God, is you, Master?
(ODYSSEUS *grabs her, covers her mouth.*)
ODYSSEUS
Hear those wild boars in there? Shut up, or we'll all die!
(TELEMACHUS *enters, hooded.*)
TELEMACHUS
Is there no end to beggars feeding on this house?
EURYCLEIA
Telemachus, you come back!
TELEMACHUS
                              Yes! To end all this.
(*He grabs* ODYSSEUS.)
ODYSSEUS
How is good Nestor? And my friend Menelaus?
TELEMACHUS
Not as reduced as you. Next, you'll know Odysseus.
ODYSSEUS
Very well.
EURYCLEIA
                              Boy, sit before you faint. Your father.
TELEMACHUS
This majesty in rags. This mongrel scabbed with mange?
ODYSSEUS
Argus is dead. I buried him. Show him the scar.
(EURYCLEIA *shows the scar.* TELEMACHUS *sits.*)
EURYCLEIA
Remember stories him tell you about the white boar?
TELEMACHUS
This could happen to anyone.
ODYSSEUS
                              In this same place?
EURYCLEIA
Open your arms to him, boy.
ODYSSEUS
                              I need a harbour.

EURYCLEIA
    All you like two cautious crabs. Embrace, nuh. Embrace.
ODYSSEUS
    Springs trickle around Mount Neriton's mossy stones.
TELEMACHUS
    Sir.
ODYSSEUS
        These crooked tears, Telemachus, are its streams . . .
TELEMACHUS
    Stop.
ODYSSEUS
        Streaking the mountain's face to find the ocean's.
TELEMACHUS
    Please.
ODYSSEUS
        For twenty years this union salted my dreams.
    (ODYSSEUS *and* TELEMACHUS *hug.*)
TELEMACHUS
    Can my father stand next to my astonishment?
ODYSSEUS
    You're too thin, Telemachus. You should exercise.
TELEMACHUS
    Is that what a bird prefigured? A swallow meant?
EURYCLEIA
    Yes, yes.
TELEMACHUS
        I'll exercise soon, 'Sacker of Cities'.
ODYSSEUS
    Don't envy me Troy. Troy. God, who needs another?
TELEMACHUS
    When you've come back like a beggar to your own door?
ODYSSEUS
    Ten years of Troy. And after, ten tired years more.
EURYCLEIA
    I should run and tell the good news to his mother.

ODYSSEUS
    No! Who told you I was home? Who brought the message?
TELEMACHUS
    Love was my whip, fear and delight were my horses.
ODYSSEUS
    For hours, as a beggar, boy, I've choked back my rage.
TELEMACHUS
    The wheels kept hissing, Odysseus, Odysseus!
ODYSSEUS
    Like another Nestor, eh? Along the white sands.
TELEMACHUS
    He remembers those races by the Scamander.
ODYSSEUS
    He does, eh?
TELEMACHUS
                But now they're claws. Branches. His hands.
ODYSSEUS
    My pain's in my shoulder. Our red-haired commander?
TELEMACHUS
    I hid in Menelaus' palace for months.
ODYSSEUS
    Old redhead, who inflamed us to search for his wife.
TELEMACHUS
    And came home ten years before you. He's a great prince.
ODYSSEUS
    A rich one. Who owes me twenty years of my life.
    (*Silence.*)
    And Helen, who made widows of so many wives?
TELEMACHUS
    I wouldn't tremble if I were her bath-water.
ODYSSEUS
    You would have, then. Her golden hair threaded our lives.
TELEMACHUS
    She's settled now.
ODYSSEUS
                She's in her heyday's afternoon.

TELEMACHUS
Did men find her that stunning, then, to launch a war?
ODYSSEUS
Finally, no. None is like your mother.
EURYCLEIA
                                              Not one.
(ODYSSEUS *paces*.)
ODYSSEUS
There're bright arms on my wall. Trophies from endeavours?
TELEMACHUS
Yes?
ODYSSEUS
    Unhang them, and offer some servant's excuse.
TELEMACHUS
Like, too much smoke smudges them. That'll be my excuse.
ODYSSEUS
To polish and hoard them in case someone argues.
TELEMACHUS
I'll hide your armoury away from the suitors.
(ODYSSEUS *stops him*.)
ODYSSEUS
Be careful of the cold attraction of iron.
TELEMACHUS
Why?
(ODYSSEUS *slaps, then embraces him*.)
ODYSSEUS
    Because men make weapons they intend to use.
EURYCLEIA
God, I have lived to see father welded to son!
ODYSSEUS
Eurycleia, listen! Say you hired this steward.
EURYCLEIA
Yes, sir, but suppose in there him get recognized?
ODYSSEUS
Not if you abuse him and he lowers his head.

TELEMACHUS
Is this what you meant by being 'Odysseusized'?
(*They laugh. Exit.*)

SCENE VI

The palace. ODYSSEUS *as the beggar sits on a throne, with begging bowl and oar, draped in a fishing net,* SUITORS *surrounding him.*

EURYMACHUS
He says he's a king. We'd like to know who you are.
CTESIPPUS
Under those rags there's an awful authority.
POLYBUS
This bowl is his globe. This knotted oar his sceptre.
AMPHINOMUS
Hail, sceptred spectre and mud-tattered fantasy!
ODYSSEUS
This body is a ribbed ship that never went down.
CTESIPPUS
Listen to this beggar boasting! It's very good.
ODYSSEUS
Was never pinned by the trident of Poseidon.
AMPHINOMUS
If he outwitted a god he must be a god.
EURYMACHUS
Let's see if he's a god. Slip a spear in his side!
CTESIPPUS
Spike his brow with pine needles. Make thorns his crown!
POLYBUS
Just nail KING O' BEGGARS over his bleeding head!
AMPHINOMUS
There's wet holes in his muddy face. You poor ruin!

EURYMACHUS
  Probe his ribs with this fork. See if he winces!
  (*The room darkens.*)
ODYSSEUS
  From that louring sky, from that undecided rain.
CTESIPPUS
  It speaks!
ODYSSEUS
       A storm will darken you, shining princes.
EURYMACHUS
  Great king!
ODYSSEUS
       What I endure will be suffered again.
  (*A swallow passes.*)
EURYMACHUS
  What was that noise?
POLYBUS
            Nothing. A swallow.
ODYSSEUS
                  Say your prayers.
CTESIPPUS
  Why?
ODYSSEUS
       It fans the forge whose anvil hammers lightning.
POLYBUS
  Oh, then, next time we hear swallows what we'll say is:
CTESIPPUS
  It's the old cloud-hammerer, meaning you, sad king!
ODYSSEUS
  It whitens the oaks with fear, its fork was buried.
AMPHINOMUS
  Tremble! Poseidon rises with his three-pronged staff!
POLYBUS
  His hair hangs like a squid. Scallops cling to his beard.
ODYSSEUS
  Your tombs will tumble like surf in its aftermath.

(ANTINOUS *enters.*)

ANTINOUS
Who's this, what's going on, what's this jeering about?

EURYMACHUS
This is a beggar who believes he's Poseidon.

CTESIPPUS
Or some other god.

ANTINOUS
There're no gods. We've thrown them out.

AMPHINOMUS
But he tells good stories. Monsters with sixteen eyes.

POLYBUS
Old women with breasts like sacks singing like angels.

EURYMACHUS
A bag of wind from the old windbag.

POLYBUS
Old sailor's lies.

CTESIPPUS
Oh, and listen to this, fishes with breasts, like girls.

ODYSSEUS
I have found no rest, sir, since Troy was defeated.

ANTINOUS
What a pity, since you'll find no rest here, either.

ODYSSEUS
In a man's house every monster is repeated.

ANTINOUS
We're not finished.

ODYSSEUS
I know, I prefer those out there.

ANTINOUS
Why?

ODYSSEUS
I was at Troy.

ANTINOUS
Were you? They were all at Troy.

143

EURYMACHUS
    Right! Win a war and everybody was in it.
ANTINOUS
    And what did you do in the war, grandad?
ODYSSEUS
                                    It's true.
CTESIPPUS
    This old dog has scraps of pride. Please, don't offend it.
ANTINOUS
    Tell me, you scab-crusted mongrel, how do you feel?
ODYSSEUS
    Like a lion limping down lion-coloured hills.
ANTINOUS
    He compares himself to the king of beasts? This fool?
ODYSSEUS
    Hobbling the labyrinth of familiar halls.
ANTINOUS
    Man of many riddles, what're you babbling now?
ODYSSEUS
    He shakes his mane, like tears. There was so much to save.
    (ANTINOUS *kicks him.*)
ANTINOUS
    Dog!
ODYSSEUS
        His eyes wince shut. Each insult is an arrow.
ANTINOUS
    Drag this dog to the kitchen and teach it to serve.
    (SUITORS *begin to lead* ODYSSEUS *out.* ODYSSEUS *stops,*
    turns.)
ODYSSEUS
    Whyn't you search for your weapons, in case you're besieged?
EURYMACHUS
    Who's going to besiege us?
ODYSSEUS
                    Your enemies.

ANTINOUS

Who're they?

(TELEMACHUS *enters as a steward*.)

ODYSSEUS

An old swineherd. A boy. That swallow. All of these.

EURYMACHUS

Antinous! The weapons. They've been taken away!

ANTINOUS

Who moved the swords and lances that were on this rack?

TELEMACHUS

Me, sir. They were losing lustre from kitchen smoke.

ANTINOUS

Who appointed you armourer? Run, bring them back!

TELEMACHUS

Sir . . .

ANTINOUS

You heard what I said.

(*He slaps* TELEMACHUS, *kicks him*.)

ODYSSEUS (*Laughing*)

Good. Give him one more smack.

(*A loud rumbling noise, echoing*.)

EURYMACHUS

What was the sound? What is that reverberation?

AMPHINOMUS

Like a bull in a pasture bellowing in heat.

EURYMACHUS

No. That great door groaning from dividing iron.

(PENELOPE *enters, carrying a bow, with* EUMAEUS *and*
EURYCLEIA.)

With a bow, curved like a bull's horns, she strides with hate.

PENELOPE

You know how sailors set chocks under a ribbed keel?

EUMAEUS

Before it is launched. A succession of Xs?

(*He arranges the axes*.)

ANTINOUS
What're you setting?
PENELOPE
                    The final test of your skill.
ANTINOUS
Which is?
PENELOPE
                    To send an arrow through these twelve axes.
(*Hubbub.*)
ANTINOUS
The one who shoots through these axes, what's his reward?
PENELOPE
My widowed hand.
ANTINOUS
                    Marriage? So you're keeping your word?
PENELOPE
When my husband was a young pine he could do it.
ANTINOUS
So can I, you'll see. My soul will fly from this wood.
EURYMACHUS
I'm going first.
PENELOPE
                    Yes, go first and cancel your debt.
(EURYMACHUS *tries to string the bow, groans, curses,*
fails.)
EURYMACHUS
I don't know what happened. There's something very weird.
ODYSSEUS
Don't you have a soul, Antinous? Or are you in doubt?
ANTINOUS
I'm finishing this chop. Let him have the next go.
(ANTINOUS *waits.* ODYSSEUS *steps forward and takes the*
bow, he pretends it's hard to string. EURYCLEIA *shoves*
TELEMACHUS, *hard.*)
EURYCLEIA
Help him oil it, lazy pig!

(TELEMACHUS *helps* ODYSSEUS *oil the wood.*)
TELEMACHUS
                    Can you bend the bow?
ODYSSEUS
These wrists grew hard as a pine-tree from pulling oars.
EURYCLEIA (*Slapping* TELEMACHUS)
    BOY!
TELEMACHUS
            It's as wide as ox-horns, can you do it now?
ODYSSEUS
Unless these branches cramp into claws, like Nestor's.
TELEMACHUS
If I urged the wood's spirit, what should I beg for?
ODYSSEUS
Her pliant accommodation, in spring and hum.
ANTINOUS
What's this ritual? Stay away from that beggar!
ODYSSEUS
Athena! Make their throats trees, where arrows find home!
TELEMACHUS
Bend, bend!
ODYSSEUS
            Come, supple ash! Take this bit in your teeth!
(*He strings the bow.*)
TELEMACHUS
It's hooked, the string is taut as a poet's lyre.
(*He plucks the bow-string.*)
ODYSSEUS
Well, let's hope its song brings a hundred throats to grief.
AMPHINOMUS
He's strung it!
ODYSSEUS (*To* TELEMACHUS)
            Step back!
AMPHINOMUS
                    Not bad for the old fellow!
(ODYSSEUS *shoots the arrow through the twelve axes.*)

147

PENELOPE
This beggar has won. He will inherit this house.
EUMAEUS
Eurycleia, this isn't safe. Take her now. Please!
PENELOPE
But my vow.
EUMAEUS
                    Was made to princes, not to beggars.
(EURYCLEIA *exits with* PENELOPE.)
ODYSSEUS
THE HORN GATE'S OPEN! AN EAGLE IS
    KILLING YOUR GEESE!
(ANTINOUS *advances and points.*)
ANTINOUS
The bow.
ODYSSEUS
Would you like your soul to fly from this wood?
CTESIPPUS
Now aim that bow steadily, you dolt! Be careful.
(ODYSSEUS *hits* ANTINOUS.)
EURYMACHUS
You blind fool.
ODYSSEUS
                    It was an accident.
EURYMACHUS
                              In his throat?
ANTINOUS
Dislodge his swallow's beak from my throat. O my soul!
(*He chokes, dies.* BILLY BLUE *enters.*)
BILLY BLUE
I saw his soul whirr through the ribs of his body.
TELEMACHUS
Like through the twelve axes!
BILLY BLUE
                              The soul is visible!

ODYSSEUS
Antinous, it was better to marry than die.
BILLY BLUE
Where're the others?
TELEMACHUS
They're like shocked statues. Watching him still.
ODYSSEUS
Dogs, didn't you keep baying I'd never get home?
POLYBUS
O many-wiled model of human survival!
EURYMACHUS
Odysseus! It's Odysseus! Welcome, sir! Welcome!
(*He crawls on his knees.*)
CTESIPPUS
We beg. On our knees.
ODYSSEUS
Don't you think begging is vile?
(*He kills* EURYMACHUS. *The other* SUITORS *run.*
EUMAEUS *gives* ODYSSEUS *the shield.*)
EUMAEUS
Here, you cunning tortoise! You forgot your buckler.
ODYSSEUS
This turtle took ten years, Ajax, but it's ashore.
EUMAEUS
To hide your head when lances fly. Well, three of us.
TELEMACHUS
If we had Troy's trim captain here, a hundred to four.
(*Noise of the* SUITORS.)
EUMAEUS
A hundred murmurs, like wind lifting a forest.
ODYSSEUS
Like a green wave gathering, assembling its charge.
TELEMACHUS
Where's that goddess or captain now?
(*Screeching of birds.*)

149

EUMAEUS

There! In that nest!

TELEMACHUS
The screech of the swallow-nation, Athena's rage.

ODYSSEUS (*To the birds*)
Swoop from that roof-tree, friends! Snatch the eggs of their
eyes!
(*Shadows of swallows crossing.*)

EUMAEUS
The breaker's pluming, it's going to burst through that door.

ODYSSEUS
If its force swirls us apart, bless you, Eumaeus!

EUMAEUS
They sound like that white river when we raced the boar.
(*The hundred* SUITORS *charge. The swallows attack their
eyes.* ODYSSEUS *with the bow,* EUMAEUS *with buckler and
sword,* TELEMACHUS *with his lance kill the hundred*
SUITORS. EURYCLEIA *enters.*)

EUMAEUS
A black howl of triumph for the slain is custom.

BILLY BLUE
To lift their souls cloud-ward, like rooks beating black sails.

EUMAEUS
Wheel like a cyclone, a sybil spun by a storm!

EURYCLEIA
No, no!

BILLY BLUE
Cry! Woman, your breath will unfurl their souls.
(*Rising wind, darkness.* EURYCLEIA *cowls herself, whirls, a
long howl.*)

TELEMACHUS
How odd is this excess of silence! Not a breath.

ODYSSEUS
When I look at them I hear armour and chaos.

TELEMACHUS
Quiet as a hundred brides whose suitor is death.

(*War noises increasing. The* SUITORS *begin to stir.*)
ODYSSEUS
 Look! Nestor, Thersites, my silent Greek chorus.
TELEMACHUS
 But you can talk to me, Father. Father, you're home.
ODYSSEUS
 Then who are those soundless shadows crossing my wall?
TELEMACHUS
 What is he staring at? Eumaeus, help him!
ODYSSEUS
 Look! I will not fight the Trojans! My mind's not well.
EUMAEUS
 This is a madness that I've seen on him before.
TELEMACHUS
 When?
EUMAEUS
       When you were a baby. It's back with him now.
TELEMACHUS
 What happened?
EUMAEUS
       A test. They laid you on a furrow.
TELEMACHUS
 In a field?
EUMAEUS
       He stopped. You were inches from his plough.
ODYSSEUS
 Look! (*Points at the* SUITORS.)
       Troy's mulch. Troy's rain! Wounds. Festering diseases!
BILLY BLUE
 Troy's glory.
ODYSSEUS
       I'll kill you for telling boys that lie!
 (*He leaps towards* BILLY BLUE, *grabs him.*)
EUMAEUS
 He's a homeless, wandering voice, Odysseus.
 (*Pause.*)

Kill him and you stain the fountain of poetry.
(*The* SUITORS *rise, as* WARRIORS.)
BILLY BLUE
His mind's dislodged from its masonry. From Troy's wall.
ODYSSEUS
Crouched shadows in starlight. Foaled from a wooden horse.
TELEMACHUS
Father . . .
ODYSSEUS
          Over dead stones, I heard Hecuba wail.
EUMAEUS
Wait. This is the after-shock that is war's remorse.
(ODYSSEUS *stumbles over* ANTINOUS' *body.*)
ODYSSEUS
Now why has the tide dragged this log into my house?
TELEMACHUS
This is Antinous! Not a log. Rather, it was.
ODYSSEUS
The spitting image of Ajax. The same hooked nose.
EUMAEUS
This is not Ajax.
ODYSSEUS
          Not him? Where's Odysseus?
TELEMACHUS
Here.
ODYSSEUS
     Look at him stride; arrogant, floating Ajax!
(ANTINOUS / AJAX *moves away, turns, exits.*)
TELEMACHUS
Sir!
ODYSSEUS
     Cut me, in hell. Couldn't face Achilles' shield.
TELEMACHUS
The shield is home now. The lances ranged on their racks.

ODYSSEUS
Look how he stalks through the stench of the battlefield!
EUMAEUS
These images rise from the shield. They're not his own.
ODYSSEUS
Since when did logs stand, then walk leagues over water?
EUMAEUS
He's wrestling the god for his mind.
ODYSSEUS (*Shouting*)

POSEIDON!

(*He hurls* TELEMACHUS *off.*)
TELEMACHUS
The sea can't come in! Stop it! Stop it, please, Father!
(PENELOPE *enters.*)
PENELOPE
You had to wade this deep in blood?
ODYSSEUS

To reach your shore.

PENELOPE
This cunning beggar is the smartest of suitors.
ODYSSEUS
To claim his house.
PENELOPE

What house? You mean this abattoir?

ODYSSEUS
To kill your swine, Circe.
PENELOPE

And make their mistress yours?

ODYSSEUS
WHAT DID YOU WANT ME TO DO? IT'S YOU I
KILLED FOR!
PENELOPE
IT'S FOR THIS I KEPT MY THIGHS CROSSED FOR
TWENTY YEARS?
ODYSSEUS
Call out to Antinous! See if he answers.

PENELOPE
He has gone to his own dark bed.

ODYSSEUS
                              Alone at least.

PENELOPE
Hack your way through mankind! Dismember its
    branches.

ODYSSEUS
With you for a path, I would cut down a forest.
(*He shows her a charm.*)
Look, here is that brooch your husband kept through the
    war.

PENELOPE
You could have plucked it from his body, scavenger.

ODYSSEUS
The surf never loosened it. Look, let your eyes answer.

PENELOPE
This is not Troy. I'm not Menelaus' whore.

ODYSSEUS
Love, see these stained hands? I'll wash them with my own
    tears.

PENELOPE
These butchers that dyed the whole Aegean's basin.

ODYSSEUS
And this ring.

PENELOPE
                      That no tinkling ablutions can clean?

ODYSSEUS
Thanks.

PENELOPE
                      That are an obscene example to my son?

TELEMACHUS
No!

PENELOPE
To make this a second Troy! When will men learn?

154

ODYSSEUS
Bring in that kitchen maid!
(EURYCLEIA *leads in* MELANTHO.)
                          Girl, you're going to be hanged.
PENELOPE
Hanged?
ODYSSEUS
          For insolence.
(*To* MELANTHO)
                          Remember our kitchen-talk?
PENELOPE
That's just her nature, poor thing.
ODYSSEUS
                          Then she can't be changed.
    (EURYCLEIA *protects* MELANTHO.)
EURYCLEIA
She squinge up like a mouse under a floating hawk.
ODYSSEUS
Let her go.
PENELOPE
          No! There'll be no hanging in this house!
EURYCLEIA
Say you sorry, lickle mouse. Beg. Apologize.
    (PENELOPE *protects* MELANTHO.)
PENELOPE
Let the hawk fall! Let him hoist me too in his claws.
ODYSSEUS
She'll hang!
PENELOPE
          Hook us up to heaven with his justice.
EURYCLEIA
Madame, is him!
PENELOPE
              No. God. A hawk is God's image.
ODYSSEUS
I'm not a god. I'm Odysseus.

PENELOPE

                        An odd Zeus.

ODYSSEUS

Let them learn not to be monstrous to those in rags.

PENELOPE

Will somebody throw this beggar out of my house?

EURYCLEIA

No.

PENELOPE

       He saw me unstitch the shroud for Laertes.

TELEMACHUS

But the bow, Mother!

PENELOPE

                 He learnt from the suitor's tries.

TELEMACHUS (*To* ODYSSEUS)

And the tears that scoured your face?

ODYSSEUS

                       A false father's.

PENELOPE

He's cunning with intimacies and quick with tears.
(ODYSSEUS *approaches* EUMAEUS.)

ODYSSEUS

We planted an oak seed. Tell her what it now says.

EUMAEUS

Its leaves insist: 'Odysseus, Odysseus'.

PENELOPE

Leaves lie.

TELEMACHUS

He pulled the bow.

PENELOPE

            Then you helped him kill the suitors.

EURYMACHUS

The scar, then?

PENELOPE

       A story he got from Eumaeus.

156

TELEMACHUS
Are you that heartless? To enact a father's love?
PENELOPE
No. It's him. Let's move our bed, Odysseus.
EURYCLEIA
Go. You hear what she ask.
ODYSSEUS
                                        Like her bed, I cannot move.
PENELOPE
Tell me why, please?
ODYSSEUS
Our bed is rooted. Its base is an olive tree's.
PENELOPE
Oh God! I'll wash your hands with these tears, Odysseus.
(*They embrace.*)
ODYSSEUS
O when this racked body slid down astounding seas . . .
PENELOPE
When I'd kneel down like an olive, rooted in prayer . . .
ODYSSEUS
When the spray blinded me, till I lost faith in tears . . .
PENELOPE
When no sail startled the olive tree, year by year.
ODYSSEUS
The sea still shakes in my body, can you hear it?
PENELOPE
The sea is quiet and all your trials are done.
ODYSSEUS
Keep me embayed in your arms, your harbouring heart.
PENELOPE
Take root, my pine, my shade, my patience's pardon.
ODYSSEUS
Has the sea made me this ruin you can't recognize?
PENELOPE
Yes. Trials have hardened your face and hollowed mine.

ODYSSEUS
　　Shall I turn it away?
　　(*He turns his head.*)
PENELOPE
　　　　　　　　　　　　No.
(*She turns his face to her.*)
ODYSSEUS
　　　　　　　　　　Drown me in those eyes.
PENELOPE
　　They have shadows now. The sorrows of a woman.
ODYSSEUS
　　Girl . . .
PENELOPE
　　　　　They tried to strangle love like a fowler, but . . .
ODYSSEUS
　　I prayed that they wouldn't, my dove, my peace, my mind.
PENELOPE
　　She fluttered. She played dead, but her warm heart still beat.
ODYSSEUS
　　And that sea beat me with everything it could find.
EURYCLEIA
　　I'll dip cored sponges in water and soothe your eyes.
EUMAEUS
　　I'll bring the news to your father in the wild hills.
PENELOPE
　　I'll oil your brown limbs like the bow, Odysseus.
TELEMACHUS
　　I'll hear Athena's joy when a swallow trills.
　　(ANTICLEA *enters.*)
ANTICLEA
　　Wasn't this the promise I made you, Odysseus,
　　Passing their honeycombed caves, Aeaea, Samos, Crete,

　　Where the drawn shale hisses like a foam of bees, as
　　A breeze polishes the sea with Athena's feet?

　　That in an oak's crooked shade you would take your ease,

Quiet as a statue, with a stone bench for your plinth,

That here in this orchard is where you would end your days,
With memories as sweet as the honeycomb's labyrinth?

As the white sprays of lilac fall on your shoulders,
As the scythes of mowers are oars circling through grass,

Now your heart heaves, not from the Cyclops' boulders
But that your mother's prophecy should come to pass?
(ATHENA *enters*.)

ATHENA
When quick foam laurels the forehead of drowned Ajax,
When nets of light on the sea snare Agamemnon,

When the shield of Achilles joins the spears on their racks,
The harbour of home is what your wanderings mean.

Isn't this the surf of blossoms I promised you, Odysseus?
That peace which, in shafts of light, the gods allow men?

PENELOPE
Will you miss the sea?

ODYSSEUS
                                        Grottoes where mackerel steer.

PENELOPE
Will you?

ODYSSEUS
                        Turtles paddling the shields of their shells.

PENELOPE
All benign wonders.

ODYSSEUS
                                Yes.

PENELOPE
                                                Were there strange things out there?

ODYSSEUS
Monsters, God pity us.

PENELOPE
                                Why?

ODYSSEUS

                             We make them ourselves.

(*Sound of the sea.* BILLY BLUE *enters.*)

ATHENA (*Sings*)

    String the bow of this harbour tight with your blind hands,
    Aim the swallow's arrow from our promontories,
    Pluck the sea's wires, poet, till the blue islands
    Sing what you heard and saw through your bleached eyes.

    (*Music.*)

BILLY BLUE (*Sings*)

    I sang of that man against whom the sea still rages,
    Who escaped its terrors, that despair could not destroy,

    Since that first blind singer, others will sing down the ages
    Of the heart in its harbour, then long years after Troy, after
      Troy.

    And a house, happy for good, from a swallow's omen,
    Let the trees clap their hands, and the surf whisper amen.

    For a rock, a rock, a rock, a rock-steady woman
    Let the waves clap their hands and the surf whisper amen.

    For that peace which, in their mercy, the gods allow men.
    (*Fade. Sound of surf.*)